THOMAS COOK
Travellers & BAVARIA
MUNICH

BY
JAMES BENTLEY
CHRISTOPHER CATLING and TIM LOCKE

Produced by AA Publishing

Written by James Bentley, Christopher Catling and Tim Locke

Original photography by Antony Souter

Edited, designed and produced by AA Publishing. Maps © The Automobile Association 1994, 1996

Distributed in the United Kingdom by AA Publishing, Norfolk House, Priestley Road, Basingstoke, Hampshire RG24 9NY.

© The Automobile Association 1994, 1996
First published 1994; Revised second edition 1996

A CIP catalogue record for this book is available from the British Library

ISBN 0 7495 1351 9

Published by AA Publishing (a trading name of Automobile Association Developments Limited, whose registered office is Norfolk House, Priestley Road, Basingstoke, Hampshire RG24 9NY. Registered number 1878835) and the Thomas Cook Group Ltd.

Colour separation: BTB Colour Reproduction, Whitchurch, Hampshire. Printed by Edicoes ASA, Oporto, Portugal.

Front cover: *Neuschwanstein Castle*; Back cover: *the Glockenspiel, Marienplatz, Munich; Garmish-Partenkirchen*; Title page: *Neuschwanstein Castle*; Above: *decorated brewer's dray*; **Cover picture credits** F.R.P.S. (E Nägelle): Front cover; Pictures Colour Library: Spine, Back cover bottom; Spectrum Colour Library: Back cover top

Contents

About this Book

BACKGROUND

FIRST STEPS

WHAT TO SEE

GETTING AWAY
FROM IT ALL

DIRECTORY

This book is divided into five sections,
identified by the above colour coding.

Mapping
The maps in this book use
international country symbols:
A Austria; CH Switzerland;
CZ Czech Republic.

Background gives an introduction to
the region – its history, geography,
politics and culture.
First Steps offers practical advice on
arriving and getting around.
What to See is an alphabetical listing of
places to visit, interspersed with walks
and tours.
Getting Away From it All highlights
places off the beaten track where it's
possible to relax and enjoy the peace
and quiet.
Finally, the *Directory* provides
practical information – from shopping
and entertainment to children and
sport, including a section on business
matters.
Special highly illustrated **features** on
specific aspects of the region appear
throughout the book.

Decorated house, Oberammergau

BACKGROUND

'A Scots baron cannot do better than travel in Germany ... Let him make a tour into the delicious countries of the south, to enrich his mind with the variety of brilliant ideas, and to give his manners a still finer polish.'

JAMES BOSWELL, 1764

Introduction

*B*ayern (Bavaria) is a rewarding region of myriad attractions; among them are such well-known sights as Oberammergau and its Passion Play, the fairy-tale castles of King Ludwig II – copied by Disneyland but authentic only in Bavaria – and Munich, a sophisticated centre of fashion and city of superlative works of secular and religious architecture, as well as host to the most raucously entertaining beer festival in the world.

Apart from its sights, Bavaria is renowned for its colourful customs. Bavarians proudly wear their exquisite woollen garments and daintily embroidered shirts and skirts complemented by leather shorts and feathery felt hats; alpenhorns still sound through the mountains, and the cattle that descend to the lower pastures as winter approaches are decked out in the last of the summer's flowers. In the region's walled towns and villages costumed festivals recall stirring historical events.

Bavaria is a place where you can indulge in massive platters of food accompanied by some of the world's finest beers or, if you prefer, delicate Franconian wines. Alternatively you can visit the region's spas in order to luxuriate in their healing waters or in restorative mud baths. For accommodation you can choose between first-class hotels in major cities or homely inns in villages unchanged for centuries. Touring the region you will find majestic ancient churches alongside swirling rococo shrines; fortresses set over crags and defensive castles sheltering knightly halls and opulent boudoirs for courtly ladies; and Renaissance palaces decorated by Austrian and Italian artists.

Those who love the wild will find a region of protected nature parks threaded by meticulously waymarked paths, of rivers that sometimes scour ravines and at other times gently meander, and of lush landscaped gardens.

For those in search of sport, Bavaria offers Olympic-class skiing facilities and numerous lakes with motor boats, rowing boats, windsurfing, water-skiing and shingled beaches from which you can swim or strip naked, as do the Bavarians themselves, and bronze yourself in the summer sun. Bavaria offers all this and a great deal more, making it one of the most rewarding parts of Europe to explore.

At Burghausen a 1,000m-long castle protects a town whose Rathaus dates from the 14th century

BAVARIA

History

1st century BC
Bavaria is inhabited by the Celts, who are increasingly subjected to harassment by the Romans and Teutons.

1BC
Augsburg is founded and named after the Emperor Augustus.

5th century AD
Germanic tribes drive out the Romans.

7th and 8th centuries
Foreign monks convert the Bavarians to Christianity.

788
Karl der Grosse (Charlemagne) incorporates Bavaria into the Carolingian Empire.

817
Bavaria is given to Ludwig the Pious who is succeeded by his son, Ludwig the German.

907
The Huns (from modern-day Hungary) invade Bavaria following their victory at the Battle of Pressburg.

955
Otto I the Great, the Bavarian commander, drives the Huns out of the region after the Battle of Lechfeld, near Augsburg.

1180
Frederick I Barbarossa gives Bavaria to the Count Palatine Otto von Wittelsbach, whose dynasty then rules until 1918.

1183
Ludwig I founds the cities of Landshut and Straubing.

13th to 15th centuries
Bavaria is divided up between the members of the Wittelsbach family. In the early 14th century a *Landtag* (parliament) is set up to control the country and its finances.

1467–1508
Duke Albert IV the Wise makes München (Munich) his capital and in 1506 establishes the principle of primogeniture (inheritance by the eldest son).

1545
Duke Wilhelm IV reunites the territory as one duchy.

1618–48
Thirty Years' War; Duke Maximilian I fights on the side of the Habsburgs; emerging from the conflict with increased territory and the title of Kurfürst (Elector).

18th century
Bavaria is troubled by the War of the Spanish Succession, the War of the Austrian Succession and finally by the War of the Bavarian Succession (1778–9), when Frederick the Great of Prussia successfully resists Austria's attempts to gain Bavarian territory.

1790s
After the French Revolution Bavaria joins the anti-French coalition but is occupied by the French in 1796, by the Austrians in 1799 and again by the French in 1800.

1805
The Treaty of Pressburg (drawn up between Austria and France) allots Bavaria roughly its present territory and declares it to be a kingdom.

1808
Bavaria's new constitution enshrines French Revolutionary ideals of equality and freedom of conscience, while abolishing serfdom. Many monasteries are secularised.

1812
Bavaria joins Russia, England and

Austria in an alliance against Napoleon.
1818
King Max I Joseph proclaims a more
liberal constitution.

1848
King Ludwig I, who had continued
Maximilian's political reforms and
enhanced Bavaria's capital city, is forced
to abdicate because of his affair with the
Irish-born American dancer, Lola
Montez.

1848–64
King Max II successfully negotiates the
problems caused by the rivalry between
Austria and Prussia.

1870
King Ludwig II commits Bavaria to the
side of Prussia in the Franco-Prussian
War.

1886
Ludwig II is certified insane and the
throne passes to his brother Otto, who is
also considered unfit to rule and
mentally deranged. Otto's uncle,
Luitpold, is declared regent and governs
Bavaria until his death in 1912.

1918
With the end of World War I Kurt
Eisner leads the Bavarian Revolution,
deposes King Ludwig III and becomes
the first president of the socialist
Bavarian republic.

1919
Eisner's assassination in Munich leads to
the 'Red Terror' when the Communists
seize power and declare a Soviet-style
republic. This collapses in May and is
followed by the 'White Terror' during
which the army and the Freikorps
(citizens' volunteer force) attack Munich
and assassinate the Communist leaders.
Bavaria becomes part of the Weimar
Republic.

1923
Following abortive right-wing coups in

Max I Joseph, the first king of Bavaria, in
front of Munich's Nationaltheater

1920 and 1921, Adolf Hitler's Nazi party
attempts to seize power by means of the
unsuccessful Munich Putsch.

1933–45
Adolf Hitler comes to power in 1933 and
Bavaria remains a Nazi stronghold until
Germany surrenders on 7 May 1945.

1948
Bavaria becomes a *Land* (state) of the
Deutsche Bundesrepublik (the German
Federal Republic).

1972
Munich hosts the Olympic Games.

1989
The reunification of Germany.

Geography

*B*avaria is the largest of Germany's 16 *Bundesländer* (Federal States). It covers 70,553sq km and comprises the whole of southeastern Germany. Bavaria has a population of some 10 million, over half of whom live in towns and cities (a fifth in cities of more than 100,000 inhabitants). Its capital, München (Munich), sits on a plateau between the Donau (Danube) and the Bayerische Alpen (Bavarian Alps) and is western Germany's third largest city.

Mountains

Bavaria's southern borders are sheltered by the Central Alps whose peaks include Germany's highest mountain, the Zugspitze (2,963m), as well as the Watzmann (2,713m). These Alpine ranges retain snow for half the year, as do the lesser mountains of northeastern Bavaria. Elsewhere the summers are warm and the vine-clad valley of the lower Main is particularly mild, but in winter cold weather sharply returns.

Water

Two major rivers, the Danube and the Main, cross Bavaria, linked by the Rhein-Main-Donau canal. Bavaria is a totally landlocked state but it has numerous lakes (see pages 134–6). Among the largest are the Chiemsee (82sq km, see pages 66–7), and the

Romantic Burghausen on the Salzach river

Starnberger See (21km long, up to 5km wide and 123m at its deepest). Bavaria also includes the eastern shores of the Bodensee (Lake Constance), central Europe's third largest lake (76 by 14km), which is fed by the River Rhine and lies on the borders of Germany, Austria and Switzerland. Among smaller lakes is the narrow Königssee (see page 76), set within the Berchtesgaden National Park (see page 138).

Forests

More than 30 per cent of Bavaria is forested. Tracts of spruce, mixed with beech and silver fir, cover the Alpine slopes. Similar woodland cloaks the undulating and low-lying plateau of the Vorderer Forest in the southwest and the Bayerischer Wald (Bavarian Forest) in the northeast (see page 138). This last adjoins the Böhmerwald (Bohemian Forest), in the Czech Republic, to form the largest forested region in Europe. The Bavarian Forest is divided by the Pfahl, a quartz ridge varying in height from 20m to 30m that follows the Regen valley. Northeast of this ridge rises the mountainous Hinterer Wald (Hinterer Forest), whose highest peak is the 1,456m Grosser Arber. The 63,000 hectares of deciduous trees (chiefly oaks and beech) in the Spessart Forest of Franconia contrast with the conifers that make up the rest of Bavaria's woodland.

Attractive forests make up more than a third of Bavaria's countryside

The land

Geologically, Bavaria has a base of granite and laminated quartz, feldspar and mica. Sandstone underlies the northern parts, where the stone houses built by people of Frankish descent contrast with the region's half-timbered homes and farmsteads. In the limestone region east of Nürnberg (Nuremberg), the Altmuhl valley is pitted with underground caves, including the 1,200m-long Maximiliansgrotte near Burg Veldenstein.

Wheat, rye and barley are the main cereal crops, though a good quarter of the land is devoted to the hops and vines that produce Bavaria's celebrated beers and the wines of Franconia. The Hallertau in lower Bavaria is the world's largest hop-growing region. As well as this traditional agricultural base, Bavaria has a prosperous industrial sector, which employs over half the working population, and a substantial tourist trade.

Superb Alpine scenery attracts visitors to the Berchtesgaden area

Politics

Germany is a federal republic made up of 16 separate states. Most Germans regard Bavaria as the leading champion of federalism and a bulwark of democracy. In the German Federal Council (the Bundesrat), Bavaria has six out of the 68 votes. When the German parliament decided, in 1990, that the new seat of government of the united Germany should be in Berlin, Bavaria was the first state to open an office there.

The local scene

Bavaria's leading political party is the Christian Social Union (the CSU or Christlich-Soziale Union), the regional equivalent of Germany's Christian Democratic Party. Its main rivals, with whom it is often in coalition, are the Free Democratic Party (FPD) and the Social Democratic Party (SPD). By means of such alliances the CSU has governed Bavaria continuously since 1946 (apart from the years between 1954 and 1957).

The German constitution of 1946 reorganised Bavaria as a free democratic state. Elections to the Landtag, the lower house of the Bavarian parliament, take place every four years, after which the party in office selects a Minister-President and a cabinet. A counterweight to the Landtag is the Senate, made up of representatives of Bavaria's various cultural, religious, economic and social groupings.

Though Bavaria is an integral part of federal Germany, and of its central political institutions, it possesses considerable autonomy, just like the other German *Länder*. The Landtag is responsible for carrying out the decisions of central government as well as its own decrees. Each *Land* has considerable financial autonomy. In theory this ensures that in Bavaria, as elsewhere in the federal republic, there is a close rapport between the citizens and political decision-makers.

The international stage

Bavaria has profited from being part of the fourth most powerful economy in the world (after the United States of America, Russia – whose finances went seriously awry after the dissolution of the USSR – and Japan). It is part of a country which exports more goods than any other in the world. Its currency, the *Deutschmark*, is the world's second reserve currency. Inevitably, Germany

For many years Bavarian politics were dominated by Franz-Joseph Strauss

has become the dominant force in the European Union, of which it is a founder member.

Post-war developments

This pre-eminence has been achieved despite the almost complete destruction of German industry as a result of World War II. The former division of the country into East and West, symbolised by the Berlin Wall, was partially eased by the late Willy Brandt who, in a coalition with the Free Democrats, was elected German chancellor in 1969; he set about easing the tensions between the two Germanies, securing a treaty in 1971 that committed both sides to the development of friendly relations.

In the meantime, politics in staunchly conservative Bavaria were, for many years, dominated by Franz-Joseph Strauss, who had served as the defence minister of the Federal Republic. Born in 1915, Strauss served his country during World War II, was captured by the Americans, and in 1946 helped to found the Christian Social Union, the CSU.

An ardent patriot, Strauss became a member of the German Federal Parliament (the Bundestag) in 1949, served as a minister in the government of Konrad Adenauer, achieving the office of defence minister, and was elected chairman of the CSU in 1961. He resigned as defence minister in 1962 after charges of treason levelled at journalists on *Der Spiegel* were proved to be false. Four years later he was back in national politics as minister of finance.

For many years Strauss opposed Willy Brandt's policy of *rapprochement* with East Germany and the Communist states of eastern Europe, although he later changed his mind. Strauss was elected President of Bavaria in 1978;

Roman Herzog, Federal President since 1994, Germany's official Head of State

two years later he was nominated by the CSU and the CDU (Christian Democratic Union) to run for the German head of government (Chancellor), but he lost to Helmut Schmidt.

In 1976 the CSU party supported Helmut Kohl's failed candidature for the post of Federal Chancellor, and Kohl generously stood down in 1978 to allow Strauss to seek that office. A coalition between the CSU, the CDU and the FDP made certain that Kohl was elected Chancellor in 1983, 1987 and 1994.

BAROQUE AND ROCOCO

After the deprivations of the Thirty Years' War (1618–48) Bavaria experienced the flowering of a new style of architecture, inspired by Austrian and Italian masters. Using exaggerated columns, mouldings and sinuous curves, baroque architects broke up wall surfaces, creating buildings of hitherto unknown vigour – as can be seen, for example, at Enrico Zuccalli's monastery church in Ettal (see page 84).

In Bavaria, the tiny village of Wessobrunn became a centre for training craftsmen in the techniques of stucco and fresco work. Among those who learned their craft here were Franz Xavier, Joseph Anton and Johann Michael Feuchtmayr, all of whom made a contribution to baroque architecture. Wessobrunn was also the birthplace of Domenikus and Johann Baptist Zimmermann, whose

masterpiece is the Wieskirche, a pilgrimage church near Steingaden.

These craftsmen displayed astonishing virtuosity. At Prien am Chiemsee (see page 67), for instance,

Johann Baptist Zimmermann and his son Joseph decorated the church of Maria Himmelfahrt, creating *trompe-l'oeil* blue canopies out of stucco and painting the Battle of Lepanto of 1571 on the main ceiling, which resulted in the destruction of the Turkish fleet in the Mediterranean.

Bavaria's finest baroque architect, Balthasar Neumann, studied in Vienna. For the Residenz at Würzburg (see pages 124–5) he built a magnificently vaulted stairway, one of the finest baroque creations in Europe. This was decorated by the Venetian artist Giovanni Battista Tiepolo with what is claimed to be the largest fresco in the world.

Originating in France, the rococo style brought yet more exuberance to

Above: cupola,
Ettal's church
Left: ceiling,
Munich's Residenz
Right: Church of
St Anne, Munich
Bottom left and
right:
Wallfahrtskirche,
Steinhausen

architects and landscape
designers with lavish
baroque and rococo
music. Today you can
enjoy such music in, for
example, Schloss Seehof at
Bamberg, performed by the
Bamberg Baroque
Ensemble.

Bavarian buildings. Asymmetrical
flourishes, flower, shell and scroll
motifs, arabesques and festoons all
contributed to lavish interior decoration,
to furniture and even to tableware.
Silversmiths and goldsmiths produced
rococo treasures. Soft pastel colours
added a luminosity to walls whose
rococo swirls were picked out in white
and gold.

The two styles spilled over into
garden design, while contemporary
Bavarian composers matched the

Culture

*B*avarians are exceedingly proud of their *Land*, going so far as to see themselves as a separate nation within greater Germany. The *Land* has its own flag, composed of blue and white lozenges. Its borders are announced by the slogan '*Freistaat Bayern*' – the Free State of Bavaria. When Bavarian television closes down at night, its screens display the Bavarian flag, accompanied by the sound of the Bavarian national anthem.

This is a rare part of Germany where no males consider it bizarre to wear *Lederhosen* (leather shorts) along with hats sporting feathers and badges, and where most women deck themselves in *dirndls* (colourfully embroidered dresses). Both men and women wear exquisitely styled green jackets and capes. Folk costumes (*Trachten*) are as prized in Bavaria as kilts in Scotland and stetsons in Texas. The *Land* boasts some 9,000 societies dedicated to their preservation. Alongside this precious tradition Bavaria sets itself up as the most fashion-conscious region of Germany.

As the leather-clad Bavarians dance to 'oom-pah' bands, they slap their thighs and sometimes each others' faces as well.

Highly distinctive Bavarian dress

At the Oktoberfest (see pages 42–3) and at any other festival, they are apt to link arms and sing out their unofficial national anthem: '*In München steht ein Hofbräuhaus, Eins, Zwei, Gsuffa*' ('In Munich there's a royal brewery, one, two, down the hatch'). They reckon that their football team, FC Bayern, is the world's greatest. They claim that their two-litre jugs of beer, whose contents are supplied by around a thousand independent breweries, froth more wildly than any others in Germany. Beer in Bavaria promotes a warm-hearted cosiness. You can find fine wines in Bavaria, but the macho tradition is really beer.

Just outside Munich, the Alps resound to yodelling. They also echo the sound of BMWs, Bavaria's proudest automobile. Bavarians have created inventive routes along which they thrum, such as the Romantische Strasse (Romantic Road), and the Alpenstrasse (Alpine Road).

Oddly enough, up to a quarter of the citizens of Munich are immigrants, drawn from the less prosperous countryside, from the former East Germany and from other parts of what was once Communist Europe, attracted here not only by jobs in the BMW factory but also by the aerospace industry. Underneath Bavarian smiles may fester a little resentment about these intruders from other parts of the world, but basically the average Bavarian is snug and comfortable, outgoing and jovially unreserved.

FIRST STEPS

'People are so kind to us that we feel
already quite at home, 'sip baierisch Bier
with great tolerance, and talk bad
German with more and more aplomb.'

GEORGE ELIOT,
in Munich in 1858

First Steps

*T*he Bavarian climate is extremely variable. In Munich, for instance, the average July temperature is 17°C, but it can rise to 35°C for several days at a time. In January it sinks to -2°C and can fall as low as -18°C. Beware, too, of the *Föhn*, a warm dry wind which sometimes blows down from the Alps and which many blame for their headaches and feelings of lethargy.

What to bring

The climate of Bavaria is at its best in the central Main valley and to the northwest, whereas in the southeast the spa of Bad Reichenhall, for instance (see pages 62–3), endures an annual average of 108 days of frost. Rain falls more often in the Alpine zone, yet this region also sees more sun than further north.

Depending on the season either sandals and light clothing, or else pullovers and overcoats, are called for. In the colder months Bavarians habitually wear hats, some of them highly colourful,

decked with feathers and badges. In winter many people dress in the beautiful heavy green woollen coats called *Lodens*. In summer they sometimes dispense with any kind of dress and sunbathe nude.

Etiquette

Bavarians shake hands when they meet. Introduced to several people at once, they shake hands with all of them. When entering a shop or a restaurant, they greet the owner with the words *Grüss Gott*. When leaving it is considered impolite not to say *Auf Wiedersehen*.

Always address adults as *Sie* and not as *Du* (which is reserved for children and intimate friends, though both words mean 'you'), unless, of course, you have been specifically asked whether you would like to use the more familiar *Du*. Convention means that you address

The Neues Rathaus on Marienplatz

STANDARD CHURCH OPENING TIMES

Most churches in Bavaria open Monday to Saturday, 9am–5.30pm (sometimes to 6pm). They tend to close on public holidays and are only open on Sundays for worship (it is considered discourteous to wander around during services). Admission to churches in Bavaria is usually free (any exceptions are noted at the end of individual entries in this guide).

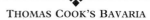

THOMAS COOK'S BAVARIA

Thomas Cook's first trip to Munich took place in 1867, followed by the first Bavarian tour in 1871. A fashion for Bavarian holidays, both in summer and winter, continued well into the 1930s, with winter sports featuring in Thomas Cook brochures from the 1920s. Above all, the region became known for the Oberammergau Passion Play (see page 90) for which Thomas Cook began to arrange tours in 1880. At first the lack of hotels obliged him to arrange accommodation in private houses. He also arranged travelling interpreters to accompany his parties.

A typical Munich beer garden

people by their surnames, prefaced by *Herr* for a man, *Fräulein* for a girl or young woman and *Frau* for a woman (whether married or not). If you are invited to a meal in someone's home, a bouquet of flowers is appreciated.

Wit and instant rapport
The average Bavarian has a sharp, if affectionate, wit and you should not take offence: the joke is never meant as an insult. Markets are especially friendly and open, and the traders expect you to be the same (though they frown on people who touch vegetables before buying them). One place where you are virtually forced into instant friendship and amiable body contact is the beer garden. Here you will sit with people you have never met before and be expected to link arms while swaying to the music.

Body contact is greater here than in many countries, and if a Bavarian bumps into you, you aren't likely to get an apology, since this is regarded as one of the normal hazards of daily life. A similar lack of reticence in Bavaria (as in most of Germany) is evident in the fact that people simply say what they think, coming directly to the point.

Bavarians shake hands firmly on meeting

The rampant lion and blue and white lozenges of the Bavarian flag

Cultural diversity

'Wir wollen Teutsche sein und Bayern bleiben.'
'We want to be Germans and to remain
Bavarians.'
KING LUDWIG I

Bavaria incorporates several different
groups of people, each with its own
traditions. As well as high German, three
different dialects are spoken: Old
Bavarian, East Franconian and Swabian-
Alemannic. Roughly half of the
population speak Old Bavarian. Next in
number are the Franconians (nearly 4
million); their region, Franken
(Franconia), has been part of Bavaria
since the early 19th century. Thirdly,
Bavaria includes over 1½ million
Swabians, descendants of men and
women ruled by the Hohenstaufen
emperors from 1138 to 1254.

Finally, this part of Germany houses
Sudeten Germans, exiled from
Czechoslovakia in 1945, who, in 1962,
were officially recognised as 'one of the
ethnic groups of Bavaria'.

BAVARIA'S COAT OF ARMS

Some elements of the arms of the
Bavarian Free State can be seen all
over the world, since they are used on
cans and bottles of Löwenbräu beer.
The background consists of blue and
white lozenges (or diamond shapes)
superimposed with a rampant golden
lion. The lion derives from the
escutcheon of the Counts Palatine of
the Rhine, while a rampant blue
panther was formerly part of the
escutcheon of the Wittelsbach family.
Three black lions, in the past part of the
arms of the Hohenstaufen Dukes of
Swabia, also adorn the state coat of
arms, while a final field, a red and white
rake, comes from the former escutcheon
of the Prince-Bishops of Würzburg. On
top of the whole is a crown with five
ornamental leaves, symbolising not a
monarch but the sovereignty of the
people of Bavaria.

WHAT TO SEE

'How can one speak of
Munich but to say it is
a kind of German
heaven? Some people
sleep and dream they
are in paradise, but all
over Germany people
sometimes dream they
have gone to Munich.'

THOMAS WOLFE, 1925

München
(Munich)

*T*he city takes its name, München, from the word for monks, referring to the small Benedictine monastic community which had been established by the River Isar in the early 9th century. The *Münchener Kindl,* or little monk, is the city emblem even today. Duke Henry the Lion built a bridge over the river and fortified the town; it then prospered as the centre of the regional salt monopoly. In 1158, Munich became the ducal residence of the powerful Wittelsbachs, later to rule Germany in 1255, and the Bavarian capital in 1503.

Palaces, rococo and art
During the 17th and 18th centuries the Wittelsbachs enriched the city. Churches and two palaces were built; baroque and rococo embellishments became widespread as the city grew. Munich further expanded in the 19th century under King Ludwig I. Longing to remodel his capital on the cities of ancient Greece, he inaugurated Ludwigstrasse, which was finished in 1852. He also founded the university and endowed the city with some of its great art and antiquity collections. His successor, King Maximilian II, commissioned the architect Friedrich Bürklein to lay out Maximilianstrasse (1852–75).

Munich's coat of arms features the *Münchener Kindl* (little monk)

City of culture, beer and greenery
Today Munich is one of the most likeable cities in Germany. It suffered heavy bombing in World War II but has resurrected itself, and you would hardly know what it had been through by glancing at the city centre today. Overwhelmingly it is a city of elegant avenues, greenery, chic shops, church towers, monuments, fountains, classical and *Jugendstil* architecture, of beer gardens and beer halls, of trams in the ubiquitous Bavarian livery of blue and cream, of buskers, students, galleries and pavement cafés.

The Bavarian capital has a reputation for easy-going liberalism – its atmosphere is almost tangibly different from most of the rest of ultra-conservative Bavaria. During the Oktoberfest and the exuberant Fasching (carnival season, 7 January until Shrove Tuesday) the city really comes into its own.

Where to begin

Munich presents an embarrassment of choice: all visitors should try to explore the old city on foot, to take in a beer garden or beer hall and to ride a tram along the many tree-lined boulevards. The greatest museums are the Alte Pinakothek, an art collection of international importance, the Deutsches Museum and the Residenz with its remarkable treasury. If you want to sample some particularly Bavarian aspects of the city museums, go to the Bayerisches Nationalmuseum for the crib scenes, to the Stadtmuseum for the folk dancers and the puppets, to the Bavaria Filmstadt for a glimpse into the Bavarian film industry, and to the Lenbachhaus, Schackgalerie and Staatsgalerie Moderner Kunst for Bavarian art. There are special tickets available giving you entry to all state museums. Beyond the centre, Dachau and Schloss Nymphenburg should be shortlisted on any itinerary. Three great viewpoints are from the top of the Altes Rathaus, from the Peterskirche tower and, above all, from the Olympic tower.

Getting around

The city centre is easily explored on foot. If you want to come and go as you please, you should buy a day pass (*Tageskarte*), obtainable from stations and some shops and hotels. Be sure to frank the ticket with the date by putting it into one of the machines in the stations or in the trams (but only do this once) – you are then free to use all trams, buses and S-bahn and U-bahn trains until 4am the next morning (see transport map on pages 186–7). Unless you are going well out of the centre, get the cheaper ticket for the *Innenraum* (inner area).

The rooftops of Munich seen from one of the city's many viewpoints

MUNICH

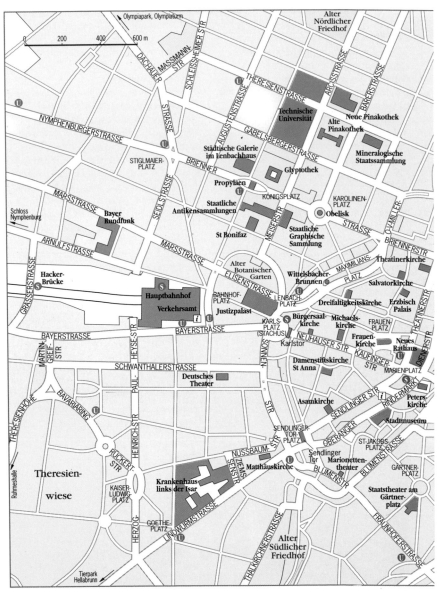

Olympiapark, Olympiaturm

Alter Nördlicher Friedhof

0   200   400   600 m

NYMPHENBURGERSTRASSE

DACHAUER STRASSE

MASSMANN STR

SCHLEISSHEIMER STR

THERESIENSTRASSE

ARCISSTRASSE

BARERSTRASSE

AUGUSTENSTRASSE

GABELSBERGERSTRASSE

Technische Universität

Neue Pinakothek

Alte Pinakothek

STIGLMAIER-PLATZ

BRIENNER

Städtische Galerie im Lenbachhaus

Mineralogische Staatssammlung

Glyptothek

SEIDL STRASSE

Propyläen

KÖNIGSPLATZ

KAROLINEN-PLATZ

MARSSTRASSE

Bayer Rundfunk

Staatliche Antikensammlungen

MEISERSTR

Obelisk

OLY-MÜLLER-STRASSE

Schloss Nymphenburg

St Bonifaz

Staatliche Graphische Sammlung

BRIENNERSTR

ARNULFSTRASSE

MARSSTRASSE

Alter Botanischer Garten

Wittelsbächer-Brunnen

MAXIMILIANS-PLATZ

Theatinerkirche

GRASSERSTRASSE

Hacker-Brücke

ELISENSTRASSE

LENBACH-PLATZ

Dreifaltigkeitskirche

Salvatorkirche

Erzbisch Palais

Hauptbahnhof

BAHNHOF-PLATZ

Bürgersaal-kirche

Michaels-kirche

HEATINERSTR

Verkehrsamt

Justizpalast

KARLS-PLATZ (STACHUS)

NEUHAUSER STR

FRAUEN-PLATZ

MARTIN-GREIF-STR

HEYSE-STR

BAYERSTRASSE

Karlstor

Frauen-kirche

Neues Rathaus

DIENERSTR

BAYERSTRASSE

Damenstiftskirche St Anna

KAUFINGER-STR

MARIENPLATZ

SCHWANTHALERSTRASSE

Deutsches Theater

Asamkirche

SENDLINGER STR

RINDERMARKT

Peters-kirche

THERESIENHÖHE

BAVARIARING

PAUL-HEINRICHS-STR

SENDLINGER-TOR-PLATZ

OBERANGER

Stadtmuseum

ST-JAKOBS-PLATZ

BLUMENSTR

GÄRTNER-PLATZ

Ruhmeshalle

RÜCKERT STR

NUSSBAUM-STRASSE

ZIEMS-SENSTR

Matthäuskirche

Sendlinger Tor

Marionetten-theater

BLUMENSTR

Theresien-wiese

KAISER-LUDWIG-PLATZ

Krankenhaus links der Isar

Staatstheater am Gärtner-platz

HERZOG STR

GOETHE-PLATZ

LINDWURMSTRASSE

THALKIRCHNERSTRASSE

Alter Südlicher Friedhof

FRAUNHOFERSTRASSE

Tierpark Hellabrunn

MUNICH

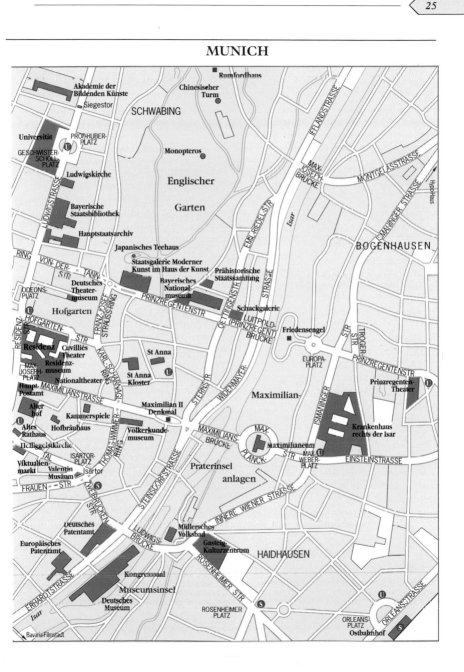

Rumfordhaus

Akademie der Bildenden Künste

Chinesischer Turm

Siegestor

SCHWABING

Universität

PROF.-HUBER-PLATZ

GESCHWISTER-SCHOLL-PLATZ

Ludwigskirche

Monopteros

Englischer

Bayerische Staatsbibliothek

Garten

Hauptstaatsarchiv

Japanisches Teehaus

BOGENHAUSEN

RING

VON-DER-TANN-STR

Staatsgalerie Moderner Kunst im Haus der Kunst

Prähistorische Staatssammlung

Deutsches Theatermuseum

Bayerisches Nationalmuseum

ODEONS-PLATZ

PRINZREGENTENSTR

Schackgalerie

Hofgarten

LUITPOLD-(PRINZREGENT)-BRÜCKE

Friedensengel

HOFGARTEN-STR

EUROPA-PLATZ

Residenz

Cuvilliés Theater

St Anna

MAX-JOSEPH-PLATZ

Residenz-museum

Nationaltheater

St Anna Kloster

Haupt-Postamt

MAXIMILIANSTRASSE

Maximilian-

Alter hof

Kammerspiele

Maximilian II Denkmal

Krankenhaus rechts der Isar

Altes Rathaus

Hofbräuhaus

Völkerkunde-museum

MAXIMILIANS-BRÜCKE

Prinzregenten-Theater

Heiliggeistkirche

ISARTOR-PLATZ

Maximilianenm

EINSTEINSTRASSE

Viktualien-markt

Valentin Museum

Isartor

Praterinsel

MAX-WEBER-PLATZ

FRAUEN- STR

anlagen

Deutsches Patentamt

Müllerisches Volksbad

INNERE WIENER STRASSE

Europäisches Patentamt

Gasteig-Kulturzentrum

HAIDHAUSEN

LUDWIGS-BRÜCKE

ROSENHEIMER STR

Kongressaal

Museumsinsel

Deutsches Museum

ROSENHEIMER PLATZ

Isar

ORLEANS-PLATZ

Bavaria-Filmstadt

Ostbahnhof

Getting your Bearings

Gateways

The old city was severely bombed in World War II and has been much reconstructed. The city walls have gone but four city gates survive: Karlstor, Sendlinger Tor, Isartor and the Siegestor.

A whirl of traffic skirts Karlstor in Karlsplatz, east of the area around the Hauptbahnhof, the main railway station (itself unexciting but a good bet for inexpensive accommodation). Karlsplatz, universally known as Stachus – derived from the name of Eustachius Föderl who ran an 18th-century beer cellar here – is one of Munich's main squares, leading into the colourful pedestrian area of Neuhauser Strasse.

Neuhauser Strasse and Marienplatz

Karlstor leads into Neuhauser Strasse, an undistinguished but cheerful pedestrianised main shopping street full of buskers and street theatricals. Walk its length to the Altes Rathaus, where you are likely to hear several renditions, played with varying degrees of skill, of *Eine Kleine Nachtmusik* (arranged for string quartet, xylophone, harmonica). The Richard Strauss Brunnen (fountain) and Bürgersaal are on this street, while to the north and south respectively lie two of Munich's most renowned churches – the Frauenkirche, whose prominent twin onion-domed towers are a symbol of the city, and the astonishing Asamkirche. Near Peterskirche is the delightful Viktualienmarkt, a high-priced but high-quality food market (a great place to shop for a picnic: the Black Forest smoked hams and regional cheeses are wonderful).

Residenz, Odeonsplatz and Maximilianstrasse

Just to the north of Marienplatz lie some of the most visually appealing parts of the centre, with the huge Residenz and classical Nationaltheater abutting Max-Joseph-Platz. Close by the Residenz, the Alter Hof was the court of the ruling Wittelsbach family from 1253; its courtyard is a tree-shaded retreat.

Near by are the Feldernhalle and Theatinerkirche looking on to Odeonsplatz, itself crisscrossed by students on bicycles on their way to and from the nearby university. The adjacent Hofgarten makes a pleasant retreat from the bustle. Maximilianstrasse contains many elegant and exclusive shops and galleries; eastwards it reaches the Max II Denkmal, a monument to King Maximilian II Joseph.

University area and Schwabing

Northwards Ludwigstrasse extends long and straight past the Bayerische Staatsbibliothek (Bavarian State Library) to the Siegestor; beyond is the student district of Schwabing, distinguished by a plethora of pavement cafés, wholefood restaurants, nightspots, alternative bookstores and second-hand shops (the latter to be found around Münchener Freiheit). Dress tends towards the anti-establishment and Green politics are discussed in the student bars, while radical artists sell their output from street stalls.

Across the Isar

Maximilianstrasse continues as the Maximiliansbrücke over the surprisingly verdant River Isar, which flows well to the east of the city centre; the street rises

The Alter Hof (Old Court), a medieval palace of the Wittelsbachs, on Burgstrasse

to the Maximilaneum, the imposing seat of the Bavarian parliament and senate. The River Isar offers boat hire and you can stroll upstream along its banks from the Luitpoldbrücke.

This latter bridge combines with the Friedensengel, the Angel of Peace monument (erected in 1896 in memory of a quarter century of peace after the Franco-Prussian War), to create a harmonious ensemble beside the river.

Eastern suburbs

Now fashionable, Haidhausen harbours the Gasteig-Kulturzentrum (Gasteig Arts Centre) with its popular theatres, cinemas and Philharmonic Hall (built in 1985). Here, too, you will find a group of picturesque 18th-century houses known as Herberghäuser and a 'French quarter'. Arabella Park is dominated by the hugely prominent and controversial Hypo-Haus with its aluminium-clad cylindrical towers, built for the Hypo Bank in 1981.

Museum quarter

The major museum quarter is north of the Hauptbahnhof, although there is another notable cluster of museums in Prinzregentenstrasse, which skirts the southern edge of the huge Englischer Garten (English Garden).

The Alte Pinakothek (Old Picture Gallery) is one of the best art galleries in the world

ÄGYPTISCHE KUNST
(State Collection of Egyptian Art)

This absorbing and representative survey of Egyptian art was begun by the Wittelsbach family and is housed within the Residenz (see pages 46–7). It includes statues and figures of kings and deities, religious artefacts and gold treasures from the Early, Middle and Late Dynasties and items from the ancient Roman palace of the Emperor Hadrian.

Residenz, Max-Joseph-Platz 3. Tel: 298546. Open: Tuesday to Friday 9am–4pm, Saturday and Sunday 10am–5pm, also Tuesday 7–9pm. Closed: Monday. Admission charge (Sunday and holidays free). U-Bahn 3, 4, 5 and 6 to Odeonsplatz; S-Bahn to Marienplatz; tram 19; bus 53.

ALTE PINAKOTHEK
(Old Picture Gallery)

Opened in 1838, the Alte Pinakothek rates among the world's greatest art galleries. Originally based around a set of paintings commissioned by Duke Wilhelm IV of Bavaria in the 16th century, its resurrection from the ashes following wartime destruction has been a symbol of Munich's renaissance.

Although there is too much here for a single visit, the user-friendly layout – organised by country and period – makes it easy to comprehend the scope of the collection, which concentrates on European art from the Middle Ages to the 18th century.

Among the German masters are the instantly recognisable works of Albrecht Dürer, notably *The Four Apostles (Vier Apostel)*, *The Baumgärtner Altar* and *Self Portrait*. One of Dürer's greatest contemporaries was Matthias Grünewald: see, for example, his picture *The Mocking of Christ (Verspottung Christi)*. The Dutch and Flemish collection features a virtually unrivalled set of paintings by Peter Paul Rubens, including the *Self Portait with his Wife in the Arbor* and the huge *Great Last*

Judgement. Pieter Brueghel's *Fool's Paradise* was painted in 1567 to rally popular support against a Spanish military occupation.

Italian representation is succinct but choice, with a haunting trio of Madonna portraits by Raphael, a *pietà* by Botticelli, a *Virgin and Child* (controversially restored) by Leonardo da Vinci and a superb altarpiece by Tiepolo among others. French masterpieces include the idealised Arcadian landscapes of Claude Lorrain and Nicolas Poussin. See also the **Neue Pinakothek** (page 40).
Barerstrasse 27. Tel: 238 05215. Closed until the end of 1997 for restoration. U-Bahn 2 to Königsplatz; tram 18 to Pinakothek; bus 53.

Above: The Glyptothek has a splendid collection of antiquities including (below) this ancient Greek helmet of bronze dating to 500BC

ANTIKENSAMMLUNGEN (State Collection of Classical Art) and GLYPTOTHEK

Both museums owe their provenance to Ludwig I who, during the early 19th century, toured the ancient world seeking out items for the collections. The result is a rich and eye-catching collection of classical art. Highlights of the Antikensammlungen are the Etruscan jewellery and the superb Greek decorative vases and urns.

Across the square the cool, classical architecture of Leo von Klenze's Glyptothek is an apt purpose-built setting for a museum devoted to statuary and sculpture; the highlight is the pediment from the Aphaia Temple in Aegina (505–485BC). Also not to be missed is the *Barberini Faun*.
Königsplatz 1 and 3. Tel: 598359 (Antikensammlungen) and 286100 (Glyptothek). Open: (Antikensammlungen) Tuesday and Thursday to Sunday 10am–4.30pm, Wednesday noon–8.30pm; (Glyptothek) Tuesday, Wednesday, and

Friday to Sunday 10am– 4.30pm, Thursday noon–8.30pm. Closed: Monday. Admission charge, except Sundays and holidays. U-Bahn 2 to Königsplatz; tram 18.

The entrance to the Asamkirche (left) and
the lavishly decorated and gilded interior with
its magnificent ceiling fresco (right)

ASAMKIRCHE (Asam Church)

This glorious rococo building is named
after its brilliant architects, the brothers
Ägid Quirin Asam (1692–1750) and
Cosmas Damian Asam (1686–1739).
They built it as a private chapel (1733
–46), but the citizens of Munich liked it
so much that the brothers agreed to let
them use it as a parish church. Both men
had studied baroque architecture in
Rome. As well as being an architect,
Ägid Quirin was a brilliant sculptor,
while Cosmas Damian put his talents
above all into frescos.

The entrance is flanked by
naturalistically carved lumps of jagged
bedrock. St Johann Nepomuk (to whom
the church is dedicated) is sculpted on
the façade, along with portrait
medallions of Pope Benedict XIII and
Bishop Johaan Theodor of Freising.

The undisputed genius of the Asam
brothers is revealed beyond the oval-
shaped entrance, with its swirling
confessionals. Here the confessional on
the right is adorned with two white and
winged skulls. One gruesomely depicts
sinfulness and is entwined with a golden
snake; the other, as its golden laurel
wreath indicates, represents saintliness.

The church opens out into a dazzling
display of elliptical curves and structural
irregularity. Golden stucco garlands and
a double balcony lead your eye to the
choir, centring on a glass reliquary
containing a bone and a wax effigy of
St Johann Nepomuk. The ceiling fresco
above depicts scenes from his life and
pilgrims visiting his tomb.

The gallery altar above the tabernacle
is set amidst wildly twisting columns and
flanked by angels sculpted by Ignaz
Günther in 1767, all lit by a window
around which gilded stucco represents
the rays of the sun. Portraits of the Asam
brothers flank the high altar (Ägid Quirin
on the left, Cosmas Damian on the
right). Dominating the whole east end is
the Throne of Grace, the work of Ägid
Quirin, depicting God the Father
presenting his crucified Son to the world.

At Sendlinger Strasse 61, next door to
the Asamkirche, is the home which Ägid
Quirin Asam built for himself, its façade
a deliciously stuccoed confection
featuring allegorical figures drawn from
classical mythology and the Bible, the
whole scene crowned with a figure of the
Virgin on a crescent moon. From here,
through a secret window, the architect
would look into his own church. Ägid
also designed the presbytery on the other
side of the Asamkirche, which was

completed only after his death.
Sendlinger Strasse 61 and 62. Open: standard hours (see page 18). U-Bahn 3 and 6 to Sendlinger Tor; bus 56.

'BAVARIA' AND THE RUHMESHALLE

Here is a massive and unmistakable statement of Bavarian patriotism. Built on a ridge above the Theresienwiese (site of the Oktoberfest – see pages 42–3), Leopold von Klenze's classical Ruhmeshalle (Hall of Fame) is overshadowed by the colossal bronze statue of *Bavaria*, cast in 1850 to the design of Ludwig Schwanthaler. Inside the Doric-style Ruhmeshalle are busts of several eminent Bavarians.

Bavaria, who stands 18m high and weighs 78 tonnes, is dressed in a bear-skin and accompanied by a pet lion. Inside her, 130 steps lead up to the head, through whose empty eye-sockets you can survey the city and the Theresienwiese.

U-Bahn 4 and 5 to Theresienwiese.

A stunt artist goes through his paces at Munich's Film City

BAVARIA FILMSTADT

Munich's 'Film City', the largest studio complex in Europe, has been producing celebrated movies since 1919. Even before then Munich was a noted film centre. The film pioneer Karl Valentin (see page 50) rivalled the early Chaplin. In the 1920s the young Alfred Hitchcock sharpened his directorial teeth in Munich with his first two films, *Irrgarten der Leidenschaft* (*The Pleasure Garden*) and *Bergadler* (*The Mountain Eagle*). In more recent times, the film *Cabaret* was produced here and several of Rainer Werner Fassbinder's works.

During summer you can tour the studios on a little train known as the Filmexpress. The tour includes special-effects shows put on by stuntmen and actors who impersonate famous film stars. Various secrets of the filmmaker's art are revealed, and historic artefacts (such as the U-boat from the celebrated film *Das Boot – The Boat*) are on display. You can also wander on foot, exploring, for example, the model streets of Berlin built for Ingmar Bergman's film *Schlangene*.

Bavariafilmplatz 7, Geiselgasteig. Tel: 649 92304. Open: 1 March to 31 October, daily 9am–4pm. Admission charge. Tram 25 to Bavariafilmplatz.

BAYERISCHES NATIONAL-MUSEUM (Bavarian National Museum)

If you only have time for one museum in Munich and want to see something quintessentially Bavarian, this is the obvious one to visit. Arranged on three floors, this is an all-embracing arts and crafts collection, including painted peasant furniture (an entire set of rooms from the Schliersee has been transplanted here), some magnificent woodcarvings by Tilman Riemenschneider, Nymphenburg porcelain, clocks, textiles, folk art and costumes. In the basement is a huge and wonderful collection of crib scenes, one by Jakob Sandtner (1572) depicting Munich at the time, another representing Bethlehem, envisaged in 1800 in grandiose classical style. Some of the tableaux show considerable humour. *Prinzregentenstrasse 3. Tel: 21124. Open: Tuesday to Sunday 9.30am–5pm. Closed: Monday. Admission charge, except Sundays and holidays. U-Bahn 4 and 5 to Lehel; tram 20 to Nationalmuseum; bus 53.*

BMW MUSEUM

Close to the Olympiapark, the high-tech home of BMW (Bavarian Motor Works) is unmistakable – the skyscraper consists of a quartet of aluminium cylinders placed together like a four-leafed clover. The museum attached to the headquarters of this prestigious company is set within a gleaming aluminium sphere and is centred on a *Time Motor* display, with film shows, engines and robots showing BMW's vision of the future. For nostalgia lovers there are plenty of classic

cars and other reminders of the romantic motoring style of yesteryear.
Petuelring 130. Tel: 382 23307. Open: daily 9am–5pm. Admission charge. U-Bahn 2 and 3 to Olympiazentrum.

BÜRGERSAALKIRCHE

This unmissable baroque and rococo church of 1710 was built as an assembly hall for the Marian confraternity, an order dedicated to the Virgin Mary. In its crypt is the grave of Father Rupert Mayer who died in Sachsenhausen concentration camp in 1945 because of his opposition to the Nazis.

Upstairs is the church. Halfway up the left-hand stairway the Virgin is represented sheltering the faithful under her cloak. Under the organ console is a guardian angel in flowing robes, pointing to heavenwards and tenderly leading a child by the hand. Sculpted by Ignaz Günther in 1763, the angel displays a slender right leg, the infant a chubby left one. Other paintings depict the major pilgrimage sites of Bavaria. Over the high altar is a splendid 1710

Light and airy rococo work in the splendid Bürgersaalkirche

relief of the *Annunciation* by Andreas Faistenberger.
Neuhauster Strasse 48. Open: standard hours (see page 18). U-Bahn 4 and 5 and S-Bahn to Karlsplatz Stachus; trams 18, 19, 20, 25 and 27.

Celebrating the ultimate driving machine at the BMW museum

A bronze boar greets visitors to the Hunting and Fishing Museum

DEUTSCHES JAGD UND FISCHEREIMUSEUM (German Hunting and Fishing Museum)

Housed in the former church of an Augustinian monastery, this is one of the city's quirkier museums, based on a theme that is a major facet of Bavarian folk culture. It is not a place for stuffed-animal-phobics – mounted deer heads line both walls and there are dioramas of animals in mock-ups of their habitats – but the 17th- and 18th-century hunting sledges are charming and the displays also include paintings and the world's largest collection of fish-hooks! Locals will wryly point out the Wolpertinger among the stuffed exhibits – a truly legendary zoological curiosity, not unrelated to the red herring.
Neuhauserstrasse 53. Tel: 220522. Open: daily 9.30am–5pm, also Monday and Thursday 9.30am–9pm. Admission charge. U-Bahn 3 or 6 and S-Bahn to Marienplatz; trams 18, 19, 20, 25 and 27 to Karlsplatz Stachus.

DEUTSCHES MUSEUM (German Museum)

This is arguably the world leader among science and technology museums and it is the most visited museum in the city. A timetable posted in the entrance hall lists the numerous demonstrations and films taking place each day and it is worth planning your visit around this (in any event you should devote a whole day to the museum). The exhibits range from the obviously technical and educational – such as do-it-yourself chemistry experiments and models of hydraulic systems – to areas of much more mainstream appeal. (Many of the captions for these are in German only, but detailed guidebooks in other languages are available at the entrance.) The museum is a universal hit with children, particularly older ones, and both scientific and non-scientific adults will find plenty of interest. The presentation is admirable, with arrays of buttons to press and gadgets to try out, and the displays include reconstructions of the prehistoric caves at Lascaux, Galileo's study and the interior of a coal-mine. You can also wonder at the night sky in the planetarium (or you can see the real thing from the observatory telescope) and explore a 19th-century sailing ship as well as numerous historic cars and aeroplanes. The shop is excellent for unusual souvenirs.
Museumsinsel 1. Tel: 21791. Open: daily 9am–5pm. Admission charge. U-Bahn 1 and 2 to Frauenhoferstrasse; S-Bahn to Isartorplatz; tram 18.

DEUTSCHES THEATERMUSEUM

This museum pays homage to Munich's prominence as a theatrical base through exhibitions of stage designs, costumes, stage props and theatrical memorabilia.

Galeriestrasse 4a and 6. Tel: 222449.
Open: Tuesday to Sunday 10am–4pm.
Closed: Monday. Admission charge except
Sunday and public holidays.

DREIFALTIGKEITSKIRCHE
Holy Trinity Church was built in 1718,
in the Italian baroque style for the
Carmelite order of nuns, after a holy
woman prophesied disaster for the city
unless the Holy Trinity were specially
honoured (curiously the church escaped
war damage). The architects were
Johann Georg Ettenhofer and his
colleague Enrico Zuccalli, but the plans
they followed were drawn up by
Giovanni Antonio Viscardi. Its frescos,
early work by Cosmas Damian Asam,
depict the Father, Son and Holy Spirit in
glory, while the stucco work is by Johann
Georg Bader. The tabernacle on the high
altar by Johann Baptist Straub is superb.

> **MÜLLERSCHES VOLKSBAD**
> This admirably preserved public
> swimming bath, with its curvaceous
> domed ceiling and original lamp
> fittings, is a supreme example of
> *Jugendstil* (art nouveau) architecture
> (built 1897–1901) located on the
> east bank of the Isar by the Ludwigs-
> brücke (just north of the Deutsches
> Museum).

Another altar, to the right of the high
altar, has sculptures of St John and St
Paul made in the 1720s by Andreas
Faistenberger.
Pacellistrasse. Open: standard hours (see
page 18). U-Bahn 4 and 5 or S-Bahn to
Karlsplatz Stachus; tram 19.

The Deutsches Museum displays technology

ENGLISCHER GARTEN
(English Garden)
The city's breathing space

This garden is, in fact, one of the world's largest city parks, extending for some 5km and covering 373 hectares. It is remarkably countrified and a great weekend retreat for picnickers, families and sunbathers – be prepared for the fact that Munich's citizens have a liberal attitude towards nudity and think nothing of stripping off to sunbathe. The grass grows long and unkempt, speckled yellow by dandelions; it all looks like parkland somewhat gone to seed, but its informality is part of its charm.

English origins

Munich owes its English Garden to Benjamin Thompson, an American-born soldier who entered the service of the Elector Karl Theodor in 1798 and speedily reformed the Bavarian army, making numerous contributions in

The informally landscaped glades of the Englischer Garten

fields as diverse as agriculture and provision for the poor. Ennobled in 1792, he took the name Count Rumford. In 1789 he persuaded the elector to transform the marsh north of the Residenz into a park, following the pattern of 18th-century Romantic English gardens – man imitating and improving upon nature.

Its Chinesischer Turm (Chinese Tower), built in 1789 and modelled on the Pagoda in London's Kew Gardens, is today surrounded by a very popular beer garden where, on Sundays, Bavarian oom-pah bands are often to be heard in full swing. The Rumfordhaus (1791) was built to resemble an English colonial officers' summerhouse.

Others added to the charms of the English Garden, particularly the landscape gardener Ludwig von Sckell who, in 1803, softened the 'military' aspect of the original setting. The Monopteros, a rotunda erected by Leo von Klenze in 1837 on an artifical hill, offers a fine panorama over the garden and the neighbouring Munich skyline, taking in Ludwigskirche, the dome and cupolas of the Theatinerkirche and the cathedral. The garden is dotted with statues of its illustrious creators, such as Elector Karl Theodor, Count Rumford and von Sckell.

Something for everyone

Several streams flow through the garden. A refreshing spot is the 'Seehaus' restaurant, which overlooks the Kleinhesseloher See, on which glide swans, ducks and geese. The garden is largely traffic free, save for a few buses and cyclists and some horse-drawn carriages catering for tourists. One intriguing innovation is a tree trail which starts at the bus stop near the Chinese

Tower; the trees are identified with little plaques giving their names in German and Latin. The Japanisches Teehaus hosts Japanese tea ceremonies in the afternoons on the second weekend of each month between May and October (book in advance, tel: 224319).
Open: dawn till dusk. From the centre of Munich take U-Bahn 4 or the S-Bahn to Lehel, walking from here up Triftstrasse to cross Prinzregentenstrasse.

FRAUENKIRCHE
(Munich Cathedral)
The twin onion-domed spires of Munich's late-Gothic cathedral have become one of the symbols of the city. The vast cathedral was designed by Jörg von Halspach and built between 1468 and 1488, while the towers were finished in 1524. In 1772 Ignaz Günther redesigned the main entrance and the four side portals.

Inside, its treasures include 15th- and 16th-century stained glass, in particular glass of 1493 in the choir by Peter Hemmel von Andlau of Strasbourg. In the choir there are busts of prophets and saints brilliantly carved by Ernst Grasser and his pupils in 1502. Other master-pieces are bronze statues of Dukes Albrecht V and Wilhelm IV, sculpted by Dionys Frey in 1619. In the south aisle stands the magnificent tomb of Emperor Ludwig the Bavarian (not finished till 1622, though he died in 1347).
Frauenplatz 1. Open: standard hours (see page 18). A lift takes you up the south tower (open: April to October daily, except Sundays and holidays, 10am–5pm). U-Bahn 3 and 6 or S-Bahn to Marienplatz; tram 19.

GLYPTOTHEK
See **Antikensammlungen** (page 29).

Face to face with nature in the grounds of the Englischer Garten

HOFBRÄUHAUS
The best-known beer hall in Munich was founded in 1589 by Duke Wilhelm V who disliked the local beer and ordered a dark ale to be brewed specially for the court. The new brew became so famous that when the invading Swedes arrived at Munich in 1632 they demanded (and were given) 60,000 litres. Bavarian bands in full swing set the tone today. The beer hall is decidedly jolly, but touristy – the local people tend to go elsewhere.

THE DEVIL'S FOOTPRINT
A celebrated fable relates that the cathedral architect made a pact with the devil, who supplied funds on condition that the building would have no visible windows. On completing his work, the architect took the devil to a point where no window was in view – the devil stamped his foot in rage and departed, leaving the mark you can see to this day.

The sculpture-filled formal garden of the Lenbachhaus

LENBACHHAUS

The City Art Gallery is housed in this elegant Italianate villa, built between 1887 and 1891 for Franz von Lenbach (1836–1904), the most fashionable Bavarian painter of his day. Lenbach's living quarters have been faithfully preserved along with several of his paintings. Elsewhere the museum is devoted to German art from the Middle Ages and is particularly strong on *fin de siècle* artists of the *Jugendstil* and the *Blauer Reiter* schools (see box opposite). The wings of the house enclose a formal Italian garden adorned with sculpture. *Luisenstrasse 33. Tel: 233 0320. Open: Tuesday to Sunday 10am–8pm. Closed: Monday. Admission charge. U-Bahn 2 to Königsplatz.*

MICHAELSKIRCHE

St Michael's is a Jesuit church, built between 1583 and 1597 in the Renaissance style and later partly baroqued. On the façade is an eye-catching statue of St Michael the Archangel slaying the dragon. Inside, mighty pillars support the vault which is the second largest in Europe after that of St Peter's in Rome. Look out for an ethereal angel, sculpted by Hubert Gerhard in 1596 to guard the font. In 1587, to enhance the high altar, Christoph Schwarz painted the Archangel Michael thrusting Lucifer from heaven.

Some 30 members of the Wittelsbach dynasty, including Wilhelm V who paid for this church, are buried in the Princes' Crypt beneath the choir.
Neuhauser Strasse 52. Crypt open: May to October, weekdays 10am–1pm, 2–4.30pm; Saturday 10am–3pm. Closed: Sunday and holidays. U-Bahn 4 and 5 and S-Bahn to Karlsplatz Stachus; trams 18, 19, 20, 25 and 27.

Michaelskirche has Europe's widest vault, outside of Rome

The colourful art of the *Blauer Reiter* (Blue Rider) school of art

MINERALOGISCHE STAATS-SAMMLUNG (State Collection of Mineralogy)

This worldwide collection of minerals includes many rarities.

Theresienstrasse 41. Tel: 239 44312. Open: Tuesday to Friday 1–5pm, Saturday and Sunday 1–7pm. Closed: Monday. Admission charge.

MÜNZHOF (Mint Court)

The Münzhof has an exquisite Renaissance courtyard of 1567. From 1809 to 1983 it served as the Bavarian state mint, hence its name.

Residenzstrasse 1. Open: Monday to Thursday 8am–4pm, Friday 8am–2pm. Closed: Monday. Free. U-Bahn 3, 4, 5 and 6 to Odeonsplatz; trams 19 and 29.

MUNICH ARTISTS

Jugenstil artists of the 1890s pioneered a sinuous decorative style (a forerunner of art nouveau) in which plant forms and flower shapes were used in architecture and interior design. The name itself derives from the Munich magazine *Jugend* (*Youth*), founded in 1896, to which the artists of this school contributed articles and illustrations.

The *Blauer Reiter* (Blue Rider) school likewise takes its name from a journal founded by Wassily Kandinsky and Franz Marc to propagate their artistic ideas. They and like-minded artists sought their inspiration in the innocent works of children and 'primitive' cultures. Their first exhibition was mounted in Munich in 1911. They were later joined by August Macke and the Swiss painter Paul Klee, over 40 of whose works are displayed in the Lenbachhaus.

NATIONALTHEATER

Munich's National Theatre was built by Karl von Fischer between 1811 and 1818, on the site of a Franciscan monastery. Though damaged by fire in 1823, and by bombs in 1943, it has been rebuilt much as it was, a neo-Grecian edifice with a colonnade rising to a pediment whose modern sculptures (by G Brenninger, 1972) represent Apollo and the Muses. All this is topped by a 19th-century mosaic by Leo Schwanthaler featuring Pegasus.
Max-Joseph-Platz 2. Guided tours: Friday from 2pm. Tickets for the Bavarian State Opera from Maximilianstrasse 11. Tel: 2185 1920, or from the theatre itself one hour before the performances begin. U-Bahn 3 and 6 to Odeonsplatz or Marienplatz; S-Bahn to Marienplatz; tram 19.

The entertaining Glockenspiel high on the tower of the Neues Rathaus

NEUE PINAKOTHEK
(New Picture Gallery)

Founded by Ludwig I in 1846, this gallery was rebuilt after the devastating World War II bombing and only reopened in 1981. The art exhibits follow on, chronologically, from those of the Alte Pinakothek (Old Picture Gallery – see pages 28–9) and date to the period from the late 18th century up to the 1920s. Most of the work is Bavarian art by the likes of Gustav Klimt, Egon Schiele and Carl Spitzweg, but other major European artists are here too – Gainsborough, Turner and the major French Impressionists among them.
Barerstrasse 29. Tel: 238 05195. Open: Tuesday to Sunday 10am–5pm, until 8pm on Tuesday and Thursday. Closed: Monday. Admission charge, except Sundays and holidays. U-Bahn 2 to Theresienstrasse; tram 18 to Pinakothek; bus 53.

NEUE SAMMLUNG
(New Collection)

This offshoot of the Bayerisches Nationalmuseum (see page 32) continues the arts and crafts theme into the 20th century, with furniture, photography and all sorts of household products from the recent past on show in changing displays.
Prinzregentenstrasse 3. Tel: 227844. Open: for special exhibitions only. Admission charge. U-Bahn 4 and 5 to Lehel; tram 20; bus 53.

NEUES RATHAUS
(New Town Hall)

Marienplatz is dominated by the somewhat sinister looking neo-Gothic Neues Rathaus (1867–1908). Every visitor must experience the Glockenspiel, whose 43 bells play a 15-minute carillon at 11am (and from May until October also at noon and 5pm). As the bells peal

Built like a Greek temple, the Nationaltheater is home to the Bavarian State Opera

out their tune, 32 mechanical figures (musicians, knights, coopers, etc) first re-enact the festivities of the marriage of Duke Wilhelm V to Renate von Lothringen in 1568, then they do a Coopers' Dance, which was first performed in 1517 because it was believed to be a way of averting the plague. You can also climb up the 85m-high tower. Perched on top is the *Münchner Kindl* (the little monk from whom Munich derives its name). There is a fine aerial view of the old city from the tower, but if the queues put you off, try the less-frequented Peterskirche instead (see page 45), where the tower offers more or less the same panorama.

The marble column at the centre of Marienplatz was erected by Elector Maximilian I in 1638 to carry a statue of the Virgin Mary (sculpted by Hubert Gerhardt around 1490).

The same square also houses the Altes Rathaus (Old Town Hall), which stood here from 1345, was in part rebuilt by Jörg von Halspach in the 15th century and was severely damaged in World War II; this tragedy was followed by a fine reconstruction of the medieval Gothic building. Its tower now houses the Spielzeug Museum (Toy Museum – see page 49).

Marienplatz. Rathaus tower open: May to October, Monday to Friday 9am–4pm, Saturday and Sunday 10am–7pm. U-Bahn 3 and 6 or S-Bahn to Marienplatz; bus 52.

THE OKTOBERFEST

In 1810 the marriage of Crown Prince Ludwig of Bavaria to Princess Therese von Sachsen-Hildburghausen was celebrated with horse racing in a huge meadow, which was thenceforth named the Theresienwiese in honour of the bride. Crowds of Bavarians cheered the couple. So delighted were the participants that they decided to celebrate the event year after year.

Thus began the city's famous Oktoberfest, which (in spite of its name) begins on the penultimate Saturday in September, ending on the first Sunday in October. During that time some 7 million visitors will drink a copious 14 million litres of beer. They do so in massive tents set up by the major

breweries. They will also consume over 300,000 pairs of pork sausages, 600,000 barbecued chickens, more than 60,000 roast pork knuckles and an unquantifiable number of grilled fish (known as *Steckerlfische*).

Alongside the beer tents, the Theresienwiese becomes a huge fairground, with swings and roundabouts, bumper cars, roller-coasters and a giant ferris wheel. From the decorations of the beer tents and the dress of the waitresses to the brass band players in their Bavarian costume, the Oktoberfest, despite its international

Munich's beer is rightly celebrated as among the best in the world

popularity, remains a quintessentially Bavarian festival.

It begins with a costume parade through the crowd-filled streets of the old city, followed by a procession of decorated horse-drawn beer carts. The opening ceremony takes place on Theresienwiese

when the Bürgermeister of Munich taps open the first barrel. As he does so he cries, in the local dialect; *'Ozapft is!'* ('It's open') to declare the Oktoberfest open.

Beer lovers come from all over the world for Munich's Oktoberfest

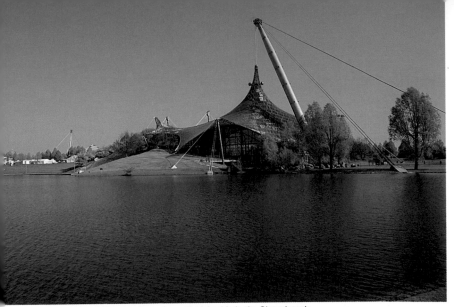
Dramatic tent-like structures grace the lakeside in the Olympiapark

OLYMPIAPARK

Built for the XXth Summer Olympics, held in 1972, this park is neat and compact, and dominated by the huge architecture of the stadium and the 289m-high television tower. There is plenty to see and do even when the Olympic swimming pool is out of action. You can, for example, visit the Olympiastadion (Olympic Stadium), a curious tent-like structure of steel netting and acrylic panels. This is the stadium used by Bayern-München, one of Germany's most successful soccer teams, when they are playing at home. The surrounding park is also very popular with cyclists, joggers, roller-skaters and casual strollers. There is boat hire available on the lakes.

The panorama from the Olympiaturm (Olympic Tower) is one of the sights of Bavaria. Viewed from here, the city shrinks into map-like form; the prominent cylinders of the BMW tower stand close by, resembling a gigantic set of engine pistons, gleaming metallically

in the sunshine; beyond the fertile green plain south of Munich, the great chain of the Alps can be seen on a clear day – they look surprisingly near. In the evening the tower gives a memorable night view of the city.

The sports facilities in the park are available for public use. These include a skating rink, swimming hall (with sauna, solarium and sunbathing area), tennis courts, bowling alley and fitness and recreation centres. Restaurants are situated in the revolving platform halfway up the Olympic Tower. The Olympic Hall is a favoured venue for concerts. The ill-fated Olympic Village, where Israeli athletes died in the 1972 Olympics in a shoot-out after being taken hostage, serves as lodgings for university students although most of the flats are now privately owned.

Olympiaturm open: 11am–5.30pm, and 6.30–11.45pm; Oympiastadion open: April to October, 8.30am–6pm (November to March 9am–4.30pm). U-Bahn 3 to Olympiazentrum.

PALAONTOLOGISCHES MUSEUM (State Palaeontology Collection)

This astonishing fossil and bone collection is more interesting than it may sound. On display are the spooky skeletal remains of the likes of sabre-toothed tigers and massive reindeer, along with curiously beautiful fossilised plants.
Richard-Wagner-Strasse 10. Tel: 520 3361. Open: Monday to Thursday 8am–4pm, Friday 8am–2pm, first Sunday in the month 10am–4pm. Free. U-Bahn 2 to Königsplatz.

PETERSKIRCHE (St Peter's Church)

Munich's oldest parish church was transformed in the 17th and 18th centuries when it was decorated by some of Bavaria's finest craftsmen and architects. It is also crammed with masterpieces of religious art, including a 20m-tall altar of 1730, designed by Nikolaus Stuber, featuring a statue of St Peter carved by Erasmus Grasser in 1492; statues of the four Doctors of the Church sculpted by Ägid Quirin Asam in 1732; and side-panels painted by Jan Polack in 1517. The Bavarian tradition for preserving saints intact and on full display is bizarrely illustrated by the presence here of the skeleton of Munditia, the patron saint of single women, wearing a bejewelled shroud and holding a quill pen.

> You can view the city from the Renaissance tower of Peterskirche (open: Monday to Friday 9am–6pm, Saturday 9am–6pm, Sunday 10am–6pm). From this tower New Year is welcomed in by peals of trumpets.

Off Marienplatz. Open: standard hours (see page 18). U-Bahn 3 and 6 or S-Bahn to Marienplatz; bus 52.

PRÄHISTORISCHE STAATSSAMMLUNG (State Prehistorical Collection)

This compact modern building near the Englischer Garten yields plenty of surprises. The appealingly exhibited collection covers aspects of early human activity in Bavaria, from the crude mementos of the Stone Age and a Roman floor mosaic to artefacts of the early Middle Ages.
Lerchenfeldstrasse 2. Tel: 293911. Open: Tuesday to Sunday 9.15am–4pm; Thursday 9am–8pm. Closed: Monday. Admission charge. U-Bahn 4 and 5 to Lehel; tram 20; bus 53.

The Renaissance tower of Peterskirche offers panoramic views of the city

Residenz

*T*his huge baroque palace in the heart of the city demands stamina to be seen in its entirety; different portions are opened in the morning and afternoon. Although comprehensively bombed in the last war, it has been extensively but faithfully restored. The palace is really several museums in one: the Residenz itself, the Schatzkammer (Treasury), the Cuvilliés Theater, plus the Ägyptische Kunst (Egyptian Collection – see page 28) and the Staatliche Münzsammlung (Coin Collection – see page 49).

History

In 1385 the Wittelsbach family decided to build themselves a new palace in Munich. Eventually no fewer than eight different buildings clustered together to form their Residenz, the finest of these undoubtedly being François Cuvilliés' rococo theatre of 1753, run a close second by the so-called 'Rich Rooms' built in the early 18th century. Next, King Ludwig I commissioned Leopold von Klenze to build the Königsbau (King's Building) in 1826–35, which is modelled on the Pitti Palace in Florence.

Symbolic bronze figures grace one of the many Residenz gateways

Von Klenze also designed the Festsaalbau (Festival Hall Building) of the royal Residenz. These buildings are matched by the magnificent vaulted Antiquarium (begun 1568), built to house the ducal art collection and transformed into a Festsaal (Dance Hall) by Friedrich Sustris between 1586 and 1600. Its long gallery is the largest Renaissance vaulted hall in Northern Europe and the walls are lined by an impressive collection of classical statuary from the ancient world. The ceilings and window surrounds are covered in 'grotesque' frescos, so-called because they imitate the ancient Roman frescos used to decorate Nero's garden in Rome. Mixed among the fantastical beasts and foliage patterns that typify this style are over 100 views of towns in Bavaria, painted between 1588 and 1596.

The Residenz buildings surround several exquisite courtyards. The arcaded Grottenhof (Grotto Court) has a bronze Perseus fountain dating from 1595 at the centre of an Italianate garden laid out in 1596. The Königsbauhof (King's Building Court) has a mid-17th-century statue of Neptune. Best of all is the Brunnenhof (Fountain Court), an octagonal courtyard designed by Hans Krumper, which makes an atmospheric setting for open-air concerts in summer. At its centre is an impressive fountain by

The vast Antiquarium is decorated with Renaissance frescos and classical sculpture

Hubert Gerhard. This depicts the four main Bavarian rivers, along with the gods of classical mythology, gathered around a statue of Otto von Wittelsbach.

Treasury

The stunning Schatzkammer der Residenz (Residence treasury) is used to display the 'household jewels' of the Wittelsbach family, along with a number of religious treasures from Bavarian churches and monasteries. Among the earliest works is a Romanesque crucifix (made around 1006) that belonged to Queen Gisela – and one of the most recent is the Royal Bavarian crown of 1806. The show stealer, however, is a gorgeous statuette of St George killing the Dragon, a Renaissance masterpeiece made for Wilhelm V around 1597.

Cuvilliés Theater

This splendid rococo building resulted from the collaboration of all Bavaria's greatest 18th century artists. The architect, after whom the theatre is named, was François Cuvilliés the Elder who was Court Dwarf to Max III Joseph before becoming Court Architect. The ornately decorated boxes are ranged in tiers either side of the Elector's box and strict protocol was observed – the higher your status, the higher up in the theatre you were allowed to sit. The theatre was completed in 1750 and witnessed the first performance of Mozart's *Idomeneo* in January 1781.

Max-Joseph-Platz 3. Tel: 290671. Residenz and Treasury open: daily 10am–4pm, except Monday. Cuvilliés Theater open: Monday to Saturday 2–5pm, Sunday and holidays 10am–5pm. Admission charge to both. U-Bahn 3, 4, 5 and 6 to Odeonsplatz; tram 19; bus 53.

The Altes Rathaus (Old Town Hall) whose tower contains the Spielzeug (Toy) Museum

SCHACKGALERIE

Count Schack (1815–94) bequeathed the paintings in this fine collection to the city of Munich in the late 19th century, having spent his life as a patron of promising artists and well-established names. Some of the pictures were specially commissioned by Count Schack and others were collected on his travels. The collection survives as a representative memorial of fashionable artistic patronage of the day. Here is a perhaps unrivalled exhibition of German Romantic, Idealist and Post-Romantic work by artists such as Marées, Lensbach, Böcklin and Feuerbach.
Prinzregentenstrasse 9. Tel: 238 05224. Open: daily 10am–5pm, except Tuesday.

Admission charge. U-Bahn 4 and 5 to Lehel; tram 20; bus 53.

SIEMENS MUSEUM

The Siemens electronics company was founded by Werner Siemens in 1847 and was based in Berlin until it moved to Munich in 1954. This company-run museum looks at the history of electricity and its infinite applications. There are plenty of hands-on displays, including computer equipment and pioneering electronics from the 19th century.
Prannerstrasse 10. Tel: 234 2660. Open: Monday to Saturday 9am–4pm, Sunday 10am–5pm. Free. U-Bahn 3, 4, 5 and 6 to Odeonsplatz; S-Bahn to Karlsplatz Stachus; tram 19.

SPIELZEUG MUSEUM
(Toy Museum)

The tiny entrance to this museum, at the foot of a tower in the Altes Rathaus (Old Town Hall), is marked by a quaint mechanical device that whirrs and clangs every few minutes – a kind of eccentric music box. Spiral steps lead up to rooms crammed with every object half-remembered from childhood. The toys here cover a span of 200 years, ranging from the simplest of wooden dolls to sophisticated doll's houses and model railways. This is a great place to see teddy bears, toy soldiers, model cars and dolls all enjoying a dignified retirement.
Altes Rathaus, Marienplatz. Tel: 294001. Open: Monday to Saturday 10am–5.30pm, Sunday 10am–5.30pm. Admission charge. U-Bahn 1, 2, 3 and 6 and S-Bahn to Marienplatz; tram to Karlsplatz Stachus.

STAATLICHE MÜNZSAMMLUNG
(State Coin Collection)

This is a major collection of its kind, with coins from all over the world dating back to antiquity. It is, nevertheless, of obviously specialised interest.
Max-Joseph-Platz 3. Tel: 227221. Open: Sunday to Thursday 10am–4.30pm, Friday 10am–4.30pm. Closed: Monday. Admission charge. U-Bahn 3, 4, 5 and 6 to Odeonsplatz; S-Bahn to Marienplatz; tram 19; bus 53.

STAATSGALERIE MODERNER KUNST (State Gallery for Modern Art)

Munich's modern art gallery is housed in the Haus der Kunst, a building that evokes the Nazi era but which has now been put to a happier use. The building is a typical example of Hitler-style architecture, claimed to be in the proud tradition of Munich classicism but

actually more resembling a blockhouse or bunker. The repetitive white columns of the façade earned it the nickname 'white sausage alley' when it was revealed to disrespectful Munich citizens in 1937. The west wing is now used to display 20th-century art from all over the world and provides a good opportunity to follow the various styles and movements that have enriched the modern world or merely proved introverted and sterile. Great artists, such as Klee, Picasso, Moore and Munch, have whole rooms to themselves, and there are powerful works by Magritte, Dali, Braque and de Chirico. More recent times are represented by the works of American Abstract Expressionists whose work inspires many of today's young artists.
Prinzregentenstrasse 1. Tel: 2112 7137. Open: Tuesday to Sunday 10am–5pm, also Thursday 10am–8pm. Closed: Monday. U-Bahn 3, 4, 5 and 6 to Odeonsplatz; tram 20; bus 53.

A shadow puppet from the collections in the Stadtmuseum (see following page)

STADTMUSEUM (City Museum)

Much more than just a museum of local history, the Stadtmuseum consists of several exhibitions housed within the city's former arsenal, each one a self-contained display – in other words, a series of museums within a museum. One of the best displays features a superb set of folk dancer puppets carved by Erasmus Grasser in 1480, and now dramatically lit near the entrance. On various floors there are museums of photography and brewing, and a supremely enjoyable puppet and fairground museum (look for the range of facial expressions on the puppets); elsewhere you will find ancient try-your-strength machines and a gaping King Kong – which moves! The musical instrument collection features every level of music-making sophistication from African bongo drums to the rare Orchestrion – a bygone mechanical music-making contraption which looks like a cross between a piano and an antique cupboard. Look, too, for the before-and-after photographs of the city, in the local history section, showing the effects of World War II bomb damage. *St Jakobsplatz 1. Tel: 2332 2370. Open: Tuesday and Thursday to Sunday 10am–5pm, Wednesday 10am–8.30pm. Closed: Monday. Admission charge. U-Bahn 1, 2, 3 and 6 to Sendlinger Tor; S-Bahn to Marienplatz.*

STUCK VILLA

The wealthy 'painter prince', Franz von Stuck, had this villa built in 1898 and opted for a fashionable *Jugendstil* (art nouveau) décor. This, together with the artist's own works, provides the theme for the museum's displays of *fin de siècle* furniture and ornaments.
Prinzregentenstrasse 60. Tel: 455 55125.

Open: Tuesday to Sunday 10am–5pm, Thursday to 9pm. Closed: Monday. Admission charge. U-Bahn 5 to Prinzregentenplatz; tram 18; bus 53.

THEATINERKIRCHE

Dedicated to St Kajetan, this ochre-coloured church was built as a thanks-offering when Henriette Adelaide, wife of Elector Ferdinand Maria, gave birth in 1662 to Crown Prince Max Emanuel. She came from Savoy, and brought in Italian and Swiss architects who created a building along Italian (chiefly Venetian) lines. Finished in 1688 (its tower was added in 1697) the façade was given a rococo aspect in the 1760s by the Cuvilliés, father and son. In the meantime 17th-century stucco artists had decorated the high altar (whose painting of the Virgin and saints is by Caspar de Crayer, a pupil of Rubens), while Andreas Faistenberger created a sumptuous pulpit in the late 1680s. Today its dome and twin towers add a Latin flourish to the city's skyline, while the mortal remains of Henriette Adelaide and other members of the Wittelsbach family rest in the crypt.
Odeonsplatz. Open: standard hours (see page 18). U-Bahn 3 and 6 to Odeonsplatz; bus 53.

VALENTIN MUSÄUM
(Karl Valentin Museum)

This museum celebrates the eccentric and humorous character of the silent-screen comedian Karl Valentin, a German Charlie Chaplin. Valentin was wildly popular in the 1920s when Brecht and Hesse were among his followers. The museum is housed in the southern tower of the massive Isartor (Isar Gate), built in 1314 as part of Munich's earliest defences. The mural above the arches, painted in 1825, depicts the triumph of Ludwig the Bavarian after his defeat of the Habsburgs at the Battle of Ampfing in 1322.

Isartorplatz. Tel: 223266. Open: Monday, Tuesday, Friday and Saturday 11am–5.50pm, Sunday 10am–5.30pm. Admission charge but free to those under 20 accompanied by their parents. U-Bahn to Isartor; trams 18 and 20.

VÖLKERKUNDEMUSEUM
(State Ethnological Museum)

This museum displays an absorbing miscellany of ethnic bits and pieces from outside Europe, including some spectacular works of folk art, intriguing everyday objects and fine religious artefacts.

Maximilianstrasse 42. Tel: 228 5506.

Closed for restoration during 1996 and early 1997. U-Bahn 4 and 5 to Lehel; S-Bahn to Isartorplatz; trams 19 and 20.

ZAM

Pedal cars, padlocks, chamber pots, Easter bunnies, corkscrews and *memorabilia* relating to the Empress Elisabeth of Austria: what they have in common is that they are all on show here, a series of separate little museums – each claiming to be the world's first of its kind – under one roof.

Westenriederstrasse 26. Tel: 290 4121. Open: daily 10am–6pm. Admission charge. U-Bahn 3 and 6 to Marienplatz; S-Bahn to Isartorplatz.

The Theatinerkirche, burial place of members of the Wittelsbach family

Würzburg
BAVARIA

Augsburg · München
Altötting
Berchtesgaden

Munich's Old City

This walk embraces some of Munich's most fashionable shopping streets and several of its finest squares and monuments. *Allow 2 hours.*

Begin in Karlsplatz in front of the Karlstor.

1 KARLSTOR

This 14th-century city gate sits amid a gracious, semicircular group of buildings built by Gabriel von Seidl in 1900. The statues on the north arch of the Karlstor were sculpted by Konrad Knoll in 1865.
Enter Neuhauser Strasse through the gate.

2 NEUHAUSER STRASSE AND THE FRAUENKIRCHE

This pedestrianised street is the venue of street theatre and buskers. Just beyond the gateway is the pretty Brunnenbuberl fountain of 1895, depicting a satyr spitting on a naked boy. A little further on the left rises the Bürgersaalkirche (see page 33). Also on the left is the Alte Akademie, built by Friedrich Sustris and Wendel Dietrich in the 16th century as a Jesuit college. In front of it stands the voluptuous Richard Strauss fountain, created in 1962 to commemorate the opera *Salome* by Munich-born composer, Richard Strauss. Beyond is the Michaelskirche (see page 38).
Turn left along curving Augustinerstrasse to reach Frauenplatz and the Frauenkirche, Munich's cathedral (see page 37). Afterwards,

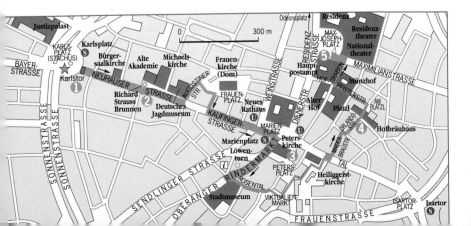

Waiting for the Glockenspiel on Marienplatz

walk back from the cathedral along Liebfrauenstrasse to Kaufingerstrasse and turn left to reach Marienplatz.

3 MARIENPLATZ AND THE VIKTUALIENMARKT

Marienplatz, abutted by the Neues Rathaus (see page 40) forms the heart of the city. Just beyond the far corner of the square stands Peterskirche, Munich's oldest parish church (see page 45), with a tower affectionately dubbed the Alter Peter (Old Peter).

Continue past Alter Peter to the brick battlemented Löwenturn (Lion Tower), a medieval water tower, and turn left into Rosental, with its bookshops and jewellers. This leads to the Viktualienmarkt, Munich's famous food market (see page 174).

Turn left in Viktualienmarkt, heading north to the street called Tal and you will find the Heiliggeistkirche (Holy Ghost Church), founded in 1208 but rebuilt by Johann Georg Ettenhofer from 1724. Its finest treasure is the *Madonna* (1450).

4 THE WAY TO MAX-JOSEPH-PLATZ

From the north side of the Heiliggeist-kirche follow Tal; turn first left in Maiderbräustrasse, right in Ledererstrasse, then first left into Orlandostrasse. This will bring you to Am Platzl and the Orlandohaus, named after the 16th-century Dutch musician Orlando di Lasso, who was Kapellmeister at the court of Albrecht V. The Hofbräuhaus (the celebrated beer hall – see page 37) juts out into the same square. From Am Platzl, Pfisterstrasse runs alongside the Münzhof, Bavaria's former mint (see page 39).

Turn right along Hofgraben, which joins Maximilianstrasse, where you turn left to reach Max-Joseph-Platz.

5 MAX-JOSEPH-PLATZ

Laid out by Leo von Klenze and Karl von Fischer in the 1830s, Max-Joseph-Platz surrounds a monument to Bavaria's first king, Max I Joseph. Behind the king's back is Bavaria's Nationaltheater, the state opera house (see page 40). On the south side of the square is the Hauptpostamt (former post office), a rococo palace transformed in the Italian style by von Klenze in the late 1830s, while on the north side rises the Residenz (see pages 46–7).

Royal Munich

This is a tour of the graceful palaces and squares of central Munich. *Allow 2 hours.*

Begin at Odeonsplatz.

1 ODEONSPLATZ

Odeonsplatz centres on an equestrian statue of King Ludwig I and is named after the Odeon (No 3), a concert hall (now offices) designed by Leopold von Klenze in 1826. It is matched by the Leuchtenberg-Palais (No 4), which Klenze built a year later for the Duke of Leuchtenberg. Between them, further back in Wittelsbacherplatz, you can see the palace he built for Prince Ludwig Ferdinand. On the south side of Odeonsplatz is the Feldernhalle, built in the early 1840s. It shelters statues of two Bavarian generals: Tilly (1559–1632), who fought in the Thirty Years' War, and Wrede (1767–1838), hero of the Napoleonic wars. In the middle arch the statue of a soldier brandishing his standard is a memorial to the Bavarian army which fought in the Franco-Prussian War of 1870–1. Near by is the Palais Preysing, built by Josepf Effner between 1723 and 1728. Opposite, on Theatinerstrasse, is the Theatinerkirche (see page 50).

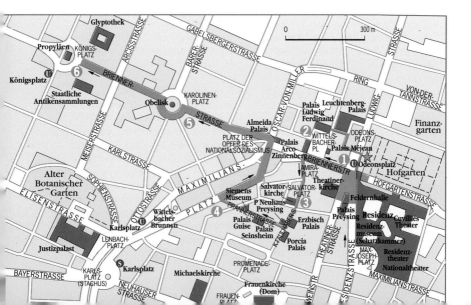

To the east of Odeonsplatz is the Hofgarten. Laid out for Duke Maximilian I between 1613 and 1617 in the Italian Renaissance style, the garden has an octagonal temple to Diana, topped by her statue (by Hubert Gerhart, 1594) and four putti by Hans Krumper. *Take Briennerstrasse to reach Wittelsbacherplatz on the right.*

2 WITTELSBACHERPLATZ

Wittelsbacherplatz also centres on an equestrian statue, a bronze of Elector Maximilian I. Palais Méjean (1824) shades this square on the elector's left, Klenze's Palais Arco-Zinnenberg (1820) on his right.
Walk along Amiraplatz into Salvatorplatz.

3 AROUND SALVATORPLATZ

Here is the Salvatorkirche, a late-Gothic brick church built by Lukas Rottaler in the 1490s. A short way further south, on the left of Kardinal-Faulhaber-Strasse, stands the Porcia Palais, built by Enrico Zuccalli, with an exquisite façade designed by Cuvilliés the Elder in 1733; it has a superb rococo façade by Johann Baptist Zimmermann. Note the pretty statue of the Virgin Mary over its portal. *Walk west from here along Prannerstrasse.*

4 PRANNERSTRASSE AND MAXIMILIANSPLATZ

You will pass the Palais Neuhaus-Preysing (No 2), another masterpiece by Cuvilliés (1737), the Palais Seinsheim (No 7; built 1764) and Palais Guise (No 9; built around 1765) before reaching the Siemens Museum (see page 48). Through a monumental broken archway you reach the grassy, tree-shaded Maximiliansplatz, laid out by Karl Effner in the 1870s and dotted with statues of local worthies. To the left is the celebrated Wittelsbacher

Cuvilliés' Palais Neuhaus-Preysing

Brunnen (Fountain), designed by Adolf von Hildebrandt and erected in 1895 in honour of the house of Wittelsbach.
Turn right, walking past the statue of Schiller who looks across Briennerstrasse, on the far side of which stands the classical Almeida Palais, built by Métivier in 1824.

5 BRIENNERSTRASSE

Briennerstrasse now runs west to the Obelisk, which was cast out of Turkish cannons in 1833 and set up in memory of 30,000 Bavarian soldiers conscripted into Napoleon's army who perished in Russia.
Carry on into Königsplatz.

6 KÖNIGSPLATZ

Laid out in 1815 to the designs of Karl von Fischer on the orders of King Maximilian I, Königsplatz is surrounded by three imposing neo-classical buildings: the Antikensammlungen and the Glyptothek (see page 29), plus the Propyläen. The latter was designed by Klenze between 1848 and 1862 in Greek Doric style and was modelled on the Acropolis in Athens; it commemorates Greece's fight for freedom against Turkey (the Greek king at that time was the son of Ludwig I of Bavaria).

Munich Environs

DACHAU

Dachau has the misfortune to suffer worldwide notoriety as the site of the Third Reich's first concentration camp, established in a former munitions factory on the edge of this small, paradoxically agreeable town, now itself engulfed within Munich's commuter-belt hinterlands.

KZ Gedenkstätte (Concentration Camp Memorial)

Today the camp is preserved as a memorial to the 206,000 people who died there, with the bleak facts about human experiments, disease, punishment and torture presented soberingly in a display housed within the former administration block. An informative but disturbing 30-minute film is shown throughout the day (at 11.30am and 3.30pm in English). The crematorium, whose ovens were kept going day and night, and the gas chambers (never used) have been preserved. Much of the camp has been flattened, but a reconstructed block gives an idea of the bleak living conditions the prisoners had to endure. The original gate is still *in situ*, bearing the bitterly ironic legend *Arbeit macht Frei* ('Work makes Freedom'), while the multi-lingual memorial announces 'Never again'. Here, too, are a memorial to the Jews, a Protestant church of reconciliation and a Catholic chapel.

Dachau town

The old town, perched above the River Amper, retains enough charm in its winding cobblestone streets to merit a walkabout from the station. St Jakob's Church (1584–1629) is a prominent landmark, though uninteresting from within, close to the partly ruined Schloss (castle), with its monumental staircase and coffered ceiling. The latter now serves as a concert hall but is open to the public at weekends in summer; the Hofgarten terrace offers fine views down upon Munich. Around the turn of the century Dachau was home to a busy artist's colony – many were attracted to paint here because of the natural lighting effects found in the heathy Dachauer Moos; the Gemälderie gallery displays works by the group, while the Bezirksmuseum of local history has rustic bygones and more.

Concentration camp open: Tuesday to Sunday 9am–5pm. Closed: Monday. Free. Gemälderie and Bezirksmuseum open: Wednesday and Friday 10am–4pm, Thursday 2–6pm, Saturday 11am–5pm, Sunday 1–5pm. S-Bahn S2 (direction Petershausen) to Dachau, then bus 722 from station to KZ Gedenkstätte.

RAMERSDORF

One of Bavaria's oldest pilgrimage churches is St Maria in Ramersdorf, generally known as the Ramersdorf-kircherl. Although a church has existed here since at least the 11th century, the present magical building dates from 1399 and was given its baroque décor in 1675. The ancient belfry is surmounted by a baroque onion dome. The rich interior, whose ceiling motifs are picked out in gold, converges on the baroque high altar, on which sits a miracle-working *Madonna and Child*, sculpted by Erasmus Grasser around 1480. Grasser contributed another masterpiece to this church: a *Crucifixion* altarpiece (1483) carved with expressive figures beneath the Cross and four side panels depicting Christ's Passion. The back of the altarpiece is further enriched with paintings by Jan Polack. Another painting of 1635 shows 32 Munich hostages taken in the Thirty Years' War.

On Saturday mornings a small flea market sets up opposite the church. The nuns will unlock the side door for access to the body of the church; otherwise you can see nearly everything from the west end through a large metal grille.

U-Bahn 1 and 2 to Rosenheimerplatz, from where you can see the church tower.

SCHLOSS BLUTENBURG

Duke Albrecht III built this small moated hunting lodge on the site of a former fortress. His son, Duke Sigismund, completed the island castle in 1488 by adding a chapel, built in the late Gothic style by the same architects who designed Munich cathedral. The chapel has three outstanding altarpieces by Jan Polack, dating from 1488–95. Also here is the *Blutenberg Madonna*, from the workshops of Erasmus Grasser.

Open: daily 9am–5pm; winter to 4pm. S-Bahn to Pasing, then bus 73 or 76 to Blutenburg.

MUNICH ENVIRONS

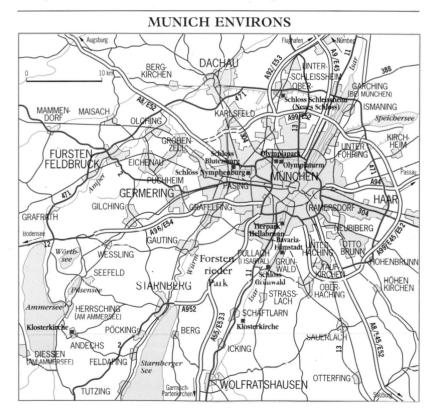

SCHLOSS GRÜNWALD

Schloss (or Burg) Grünwald, 13km south of Munich, began life as a 13th-century Gothic fortress; some parts, including the tower, remain picturesquely medieval. In the 1480s, after it had come into the possession of the Wittelsbachs, the castle was enlarged by the addition of a magnificent porch, decorated with coats of arms. Later the castle served as a prison and then as an armoury. Now it is a museum displaying prehistoric and Roman antiquities.

Zellerstrasse 3, Grünwald. Tel: 641 3218. Open: 15 March to 30 November, Wednesday to Sunday 10am–4.30pm. Closed: Monday and Tuesday. Admission charge. S-Bahn 7 to Höllriegelskreuth; buses 224 and 271; trams 15 and 25.

SCHLOSS NYMPHENBURG
The Schloss

The approach to Schloss Nymphenburg, along its swan-populated canal (a popular midwinter haunt of skaters and ice-hockey enthusiasts), at once presents a picture of striking symmetry – belying the fact that the palace was built over a century by four members of the Wittelsbach family. Although built as a summer residence in the country, it is now well engulfed by the western suburbs.

Several leading architects of the late 17th and 18th centuries contributed their genius to this palace and its surrounding buildings. Agostino Barelli designed the central pavilion between 1664 and 1674, a gift from the Elector Ferdinand Maria to his wife Henriette Adelaide. Antonio Viscardi extended it in 1702 on behalf of Elector Max Emanuel, adding side pavilions connected to the main house by galleries. Then, in 1715, Joseph Effner added the wings, replacing the Italianate style of the previous architects with one based on French models. The interior displays some sumptuous baroque decoration, including a splendidly frescoed great hall. Here, too, is King Ludwig I's celebrated 'Gallery of Beauties', 36 portraits of the king's favourites, including his mistresses Lola Montez and Helene Sedlmayr; these were painted by Josef Stieler between 1827 and 1850.

The park

In many ways it is the park, with its hunting lodges, temples and pavilions, that is the most memorable attribute of Nymphenburg. The park covers 221 hectares and was redesigned by the brilliant landscape gardener Friedrich Ludwig von Sckell in 1805. Here Effner built the baroque pleasure house called the Pagodenburg (1719) which stands beside the smaller of the two lakes in the palace grounds.

Effner followed this with the Badenburg, a bathing lodge at the corner of the great lake, finished in 1721. Each has a baroque parterre with waterworks. Then came his Magdalenenklause, a bizarre shell-encrusted mock-ruin designed as a hermitage, completed in 1728 and furnished with a grotto chapel and a statue of St Mary Magdalen.

As a present for his wife Amalia, Max Emanuel's son, Karl Albrecht, commissioned Cuvilliés the Elder to design the sumptuous, rococo Amalienburg (1734). This was decorated with stucco work and frescos by Johann Baptist Zimmermann and his brothers, and has a swirlingly decorated hall of mirrors: if you stand in the centre of the hall you will see yourself reflected tenfold.

Schloss Nymphenburg, though built over a hundred years, is exceptionally harmonious

The Marstallmuseum (Royal Stables Museum)

This absorbing museum exhibits the products of the Nymphenburg porcelain factory, founded here in 1747, and has royal sleighs and carriages: one can imagine the Wittelsbachs riding them through this great estate.

Open: Tuesday to Sunday 9am–12.30pm, 1.30–5pm, winter to 4pm. Closed: Monday. U-Bahn 1 to Rotkreuzplatz, then tram 12.

SCHLOSS SCHLEISSHEIM AND SCHLOSS LUSTHEIM

The long white façade of Schloss Schleissheim was built on a scale to rival Versailles, and is reflected in a wide, round artificial pond. Max Emanuel, the Great Elector, commissioned the building in 1701 from the Italian architect Zuccalli. During the War of the Spanish Succession the Elector was defeated at the battle of Höchstädt and fled to France, so that work on his Schloss ceased from 1704 to 1719. The building was finally completed by the Bavarian architect Joseph Effner in 1725.

Other celebrated masters added to its glory, particularly Ignaz Günther who created the east portal in 1763, and Johann Baptist Zimmermann, who stuccoed the Festival Hall and the magnificent staircase. The former has a ceiling fresco by the Italian Jacopo Amigoni depicting the exploits of Aeneas, while the staircase ceiling was frescoed by Cosmas Damien Asam. Asam also decorated the Elector's chapel with scenes from the life of St Maximilian.

The Schloss makes an ideal setting for the baroque works of art on show; these include paintings from other countries, particularly Italian masterpieces, from the Bavarian National Museum's extensive collections.

Schloss Schleissheim is known as the Neues (New) Schloss to distinguish it from the Renaissance Altes (Old) Schloss, which had been built in the early 17th century for Duke Maximilian I by the architect Heinrich Schön and decorated by Peter Candid. Today it serves as a gallery devoted to the Christian year and to religious folk art from all over the world.

At the far side of the splendid formal park surrounding Schloss Schleissheim is another fine palace, Schloss Lustheim. This was built in the Italian baroque style by Enrico Zuccalli in 1684, on the occasion of the marriage of Max Emanuel of Bavaria to Maria Antonia, daughter of the Emperor Leopold I. This exquisite building has a festival hall with a mirrored vault and frescos depicting Diana the Huntress by Francesco Rosa, Johann Trubillio and Johann Gumpp. A huge oil painting depicts scenes from the life of Max Emanuel.

When the philanthropist Ernst Schneider donated his superb collection of Meissen porcelain to the state in 1968, he did so on condition that it be exhibited in a

Meissen chinoiserie in Schloss Lustheim

The graceful symmetry of Schloss Schleissheim, built to rival Versailles

baroque palace. His splendid legacy is thus suitably mounted here in 15 rooms, nearly 2,000 pieces in all, mostly dating from 1710 to 1800.

Neues Schloss and Schloss Lustheim. Tel: 315 8720. Open: Tuesday to Sunday 10am–12.30pm, 1.30–5pm (closing at 4pm from October to the end of March). Closed: Monday. Admission charge. Altes Schloss. Tel: 315 5272. Open: daily 10am–5pm. Admission charge. S-Bahn 1 to Oberschleissheim; bus 392.

TIERPARK HELLABRUNN (Hellabrunn Zoo)

The zoo abuts the banks of the Isar and is located southwest of the city centre. It has over 8,000 animals, roaming in open enclosures in a semi-natural habitat. There is also a walk-in aviary.

Open: daily 8am–6pm (winter 9am–5pm). Admission charge. U-Bahn 3 to Thalkirchen or bus 52 to end of route.

Russian icon on display at Schloss Schleissheim

Close to Hellabrunn, Flauchersteg is a popular place for swimming in the Isar or for enjoying picnics and barbecues on the stony beach. It gets crowded at summer weekends.

Southeast Bavaria

BAD REICHENHALL

The Celts were probably the first to exploit the underground springs of this spa, where both the saline water and the salt derived from it are considered to have curative powers. Today the town also produces salt from the springs and underground lakes of nearby

SOUTHEAST BAVARIA

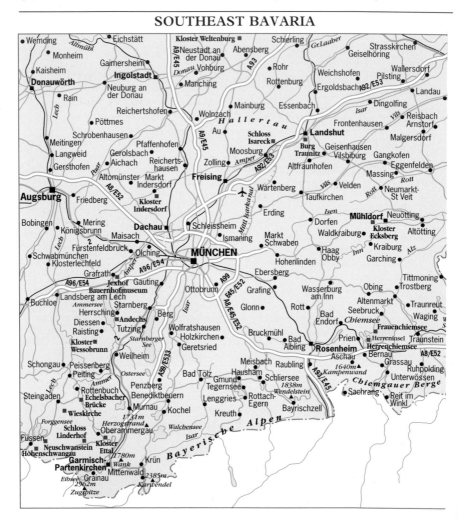

Berchtesgaden, whose waters are pumped here along pipes stretching for 18km.

Alte Saline

These former salt works were built at the beginning of the 16th century and then greatly enlarged under Ludwig I in 1834.

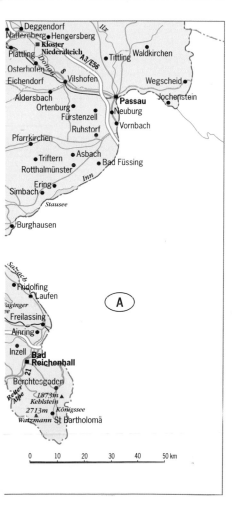

The 19th-century artist Moritz von Schwind painted the series of frescos that decorate the factory chapel. The guided tour takes in several exhibitions detailing the history of salt mining from ancient times to the present day.

Salinenstrasse. Open: April to October, daily 10–11.30am, 2–4pm; November to March, Wednesday and Thursday 2–4pm.

St Ägidien

This Carmelite church was begun in 1159 in the Romanesque style but was then Gothicised, in part, in the 15th century. Today its most important feature is a series of modern wall paintings depicting several harrowing events that took place in Bad Reichenhall during World War II. One portrays an Allied bombing raid of 1945 which killed 224 citizens; the four horsemen of the Apocalypse ride above the conflagration. Another shows the church's anti-Nazi parish priest who perished in Dachau.

Poststrasse. Open: standard hours (see page 18).

St Zeno

This is the largest Romanesque basilica in Upper Bavaria. Founded in 1208, it suffered fire damage in the Middle Ages and, as a result, parts of the church were rebuilt in the Gothic style. In the Romanesque cloister there is a chapel inscribed FRIDERICUS IMP in thanks for the generosity of the Holy Roman Emperor, Frederick Barbarossa (1123–90).

Salzburgerstrasse 32. Open: standard hours (see page 18).

Location: Bad Reichenhall is in the extreme southeast of Bavaria, 135km from Munich. Tourist office: Wittelsbacherstrasse 15. Tel: 08651 3003.

Spas and Mud Baths

*T*he Bavarians share with many Europeans a passion for health cures, and spas have flourished here since the 19th century. Spa towns are usually prefixed by the name Bad (Bath). Most developed around a warm sulphurous or saline spring with a reputation for its healing properties. Supplementing the curative effects of the water you will find restful parks, along with sporting facilities that range from mini-golf to tennis and more strenuous activities. Bad Griesbach, a spa in the Rottal valley near Passau, is also the national centre of the German golf association.

Among the finest spas in Bavaria are Bad Aibling, west of the town of Rosenheim, and Bad Mergentheim (see page 108), which prospered after the discovery of a magnesium sulphate spring in 1826, whose waters are said to cure kidney, liver and gall-bladder conditions. Bad Kissingen, in Franconia, was renowned for its curative waters in antiquity and became famous when the waters of its Rakoczy spring, discovered in 1737, attracted European royalty, leading to the building of a casino and four concert halls. Bad Reichenhall (see page 62) is a spa with saline springs that have been used since pre-Roman times, and at Bad Tölz (see opposite) the therapy is based on peat baths and an iodine spring discovered in 1846.

Glorious, therapeutic mud

The therapeutic value of mud baths is also appreciated in Bavaria, a facility offered by many of its spas, for instance in the Ludwigsbad at Murnau, northeast of Oberammergau.

Curative jacuzzi

SEBASTIAN KNEIPP
The Reverend Sebastian Kneipp (1821–97), parish priest at Bad Wörishofen, suffered from chronic consumption until he was cured after plunging into a freezing pool. The experience inspired him to devise a cure for similar sufferers, and also for those with wasted limbs. Known as Kneippkur, the treatment involves a combination of hydrotherapy and massage. Bad Wörishofen became the first of many Bavarian Kneipp spas.

BAD TÖLZ

The spa town of Bad Tölz stands on the River Isar at the foot of the Bavarian Alps and it has a noted boys' choir. Just 3km west of the town, the Blombergbahn chairlift carries visitors up Mount Blomberg for mountain walks in the summer and to the ski runs in winter.

Franziskanerkirche

Built for Franciscan monks in the 1730s, the baroque church rises above the Isar in the War Memorial Gardens.
Open: standard hours (see page 18).

Maria Himmelfahrt

This church, dedicated to the Virgin Mary in her Assumption, was rebuilt in the late-Gothic style after a fire of 1453 destroyed the older church. Superb stained glass, made around 1500, depicts the Nativity. The apse tracery is magical, as is a baroque Madonna on the arch of the choir, carved by Bartholomäus Steinle in 1611. The entrance to the 16th-century Winzerer chapel is frescoed with portraits of St Sebastian and St Roch, both of whom are reputed to be able to protect the faithful against plague.
Open: standard hours (see page 18).

Marktstrasse

Reached at the top of the town through a gateway dated 1353, the spa's traffic-free main street passes between ancient houses with rich façades and overhanging roofs. A World War I memorial is decorated with reliefs depicting the exploits of the town's 16th-century hero, Kaspar von Winzerer, who takes King François I of France prisoner, jousts with Emperor Max I and is finally slain in a tournament of 1552. A fourth panel shows Napoleon III of France in flight from Sedan in 1870.

The cobbled and traffic-free main street in the spa town of Bad Tölz

Location: Bad Tölz is 40km south of Munich. Tourist office: Ludwigstrasse 11. Tel: 08041 70071.

Just outside the town, on the road northeast to Holzkirchen, a signpost directs you off the Bundesstrasse 13 road to Sachsenkam and Kloster Reutberg. Here you will find a monastic church built in the early 1730s, whose *Madonna and Child* came from Loreto in Italy. There is also a former monastic brewery whose beer can still be sampled at the nearby Bräustüberl (Beer Hall).

BERCHTESGADEN

Unjustly remembered as the place where Adolf Hitler had his mountain retreat (and many tourist shops still make a good living selling books with photographs of the Führer and his Nazi cronies visiting the region), Berchtesgaden is, in fact, a medieval town surrounded by nine Alpine peaks of which the 2,713m-high Watzmann is the second highest in Germany.

Königliches Schloss Berchtesgaden

A former monastery, Berchtesgaden's castle then became the principal seat of the town's rulers before finally passing into the hands of the Wittelsbach family in 1810. Guided tours begin with the Romanesque cloister and take you through rooms containing statues by Tilman Riemenschneider and Erasmus Grasser, paintings by Cranach the Elder and memorabilia of the Wittelsbach dynasty.

Marktplatz. Open: Easter to 20 September, Sunday to Friday 10am–1pm and 2–5pm; 1 October to Easter, Monday to Friday only. Closed on bank holidays. Tel: 08652 2085. Admission charge.

UNDERGROUND MINES

An enthralling treat is a visit to the underground salt mines at Bergwerkallee where the miners act as guides, helping you to dress in miners' protective clothing, slide down a chute, travel on a little train and float across an underground lake. *Guided tours: May to mid-October, daily 8.30am–5pm, otherwise Monday to Saturday 12.30–3.30pm. Tel: 08652 60020. Admission charge.*

Marktplatz

The triangular market square of Berchtesgaden is flanked by painted Renaissance and baroque houses and centres on an 1860s fountain.

St Maria am Anger

This church was built between 1488 and 1519 (tower 1682) and contains some superb sculptures. It stands next to a graveyard where the first tomb on the right is that of Anton Adler who died in 1822 at the great age of 117.
On-Imhof-Strasse. Open: standard hours (see page 18).

Stiftskirche St Peter und St Johannes

The former church of St Peter and St John has symmetrical 13th-century towers (with 19th-century spires). Through its 12th-century Romanesque entrance you reach a nave built around 1200 and a choir added 100 years later, the whole topped by lovely Gothic vaulting. Look out for a sculpted Romanesque holy water stoup, and the red marble tombs of the provosts who ruled Berchtesgaden until the Wittelsbach family took over.

Location: Berchtesgaden is 147km southeast of Munich. Tourist office: Königsseestrasse 2. Tel: 08652 9670.

CHIEMSEE

With a surface area of 82sq km, Chiemsee is the largest lake in Bavaria. Its banks are sheltered by wooded hills and rich pastures rising to the Alps. Of the islands which dot the lake, the **Herreninsel** (Men's Island) is the largest. Here a Benedictine monastery was founded in the 8th century that flourished until 1803, though all that remains today is the Gothic church and

LAKE FISH

The fishermen of the Fraueninsel fish the lake in the morning; their families smoke the catch in the afternoon and then sell it from their homes, wrapped in paper napkins and ready to eat. Look out for the notice directing you to 'Pollfischer Febern'.

Snowy peaks rise in the crystal clear air of alpine Berchtesgaden

the 'old palace' with its imperial hall. On the same island is Schloss Herrenchiemsee, the unfinished replica of the Château of Versailles built for King Ludwig II (see page 94). The buildings include the fabulous Hall of Mirrors, a monumental staircase, a huge circular bathroom and the gilded royal bedchamber (guided tours: April to September 9am–5pm, 10am–4pm rest of the year; admission charge).

The **Fraueninsel** (Women's Island) is so-called after the Benedictine nunnery, founded in the 8th century, whose nuns still distil and sell a liqueur of their own. Their chapel, rebuilt in the 12th century, has an 8th-century door-knocker. Inside are 11 baroque altars. North of this chapel rises the Torhalle, a stone gatehouse built around 860, whose upper storey is decorated with modern reproductions of medieval frescos (open: May to October, 11am–6pm).

Of the towns surrounding the lake the loveliest is **Prien am Chiemsee**, whose baroque church of Maria Himmelfahrt (decorated by Johann Baptist Zimmermann) has a separate Gothic, onion-domed baptistry (open: standard hours – see page 18). From the railway station two late-19th-century steam trains run along a single-line track carrying visitors to the harbour. From

here you can have a choice of three different boat trips which will take you to one or both of the main islands, or to the other attractive towns set beside the lake.

Location: Chiemsee lies 90km east of Munich. Tourist office: Alte Rathausstrasse 11, Prien am Chiemsee. Tel: 08051 2280 or 08051 69050.

Beautifully maintained buildings in Freising

ERDING

The 17th-century feel of this little town derives from the fact that many of its buildings were razed in a fire of 1648. Only one medieval gateway, built around 1500 with a later onion dome, remains, as do a few remnants of the 14th-century defensive wall. The Heiliggeistspital, a hospice founded in 1444, stands to the south of this gateway, alongside its medieval chapel (with a high altar of 1793). One of the first buildings to be restored after the fire was the Rathaus, the little town hall in Landshuterstrasse that was formerly home to the Counts of Preysing. St Johannes, the town's parish church, is a magnificent 14th- and 15th-century Gothic basilica built of brick. *30km northeast of Munich. Tourist office: Landshuterstrasse 2. Tel: 08122 4080.*

FREISING

Freising was formerly the seat of the archbishop who is now based in Munich, hence the superb cathedral. Benedictine monks set up one of the world's oldest breweries here in the 11th century. Set on a hill above the River Isar, the cathedral (Dom) was begun in the mid-12th century and was richly decorated by the Asam brothers in the 1720s. Its high altar is a Renaissance gem of 1625. In the Romanesque crypt lie the bones of the 8th-century missionary St Korbinian, to whom (along with the Virgin Mary) the cathedral is dedicated. The church rises in a close filled with exquisite old buildings (open: standard hours – see page 18).

The Diocesan Museum has sculptures by Erasmus Grasser and Hans Leinberger, paintings by Jan Polack and a gallery of baroque paintings (open: daily 10am–5pm; closed: Monday). *30km north of Munich. Tourist office: Stadtverwaltung, Marienplatz 7. Tel: 08161 54122.*

LANDSHUT

Dominated by Traunitz Castle, which sits on a ridge above the town, this former capital of Lower Bavaria lies on the banks of the River Isar surrounded by forested hills. At the heart of the modern city is the old city, a medieval and Renaissance pearl, whose two main streets, the Altstadt and the Neustadt, run parallel to each other, connected by narrow alleys.

Altstadt is lined by fine step-gabled 15th- and 16th-century houses and several arcaded courtyards. One of its principal buildings is the Rathaus, the three-gabled town hall formed from three medieval houses. The 19th-century frescos inside illustrate the lavish wedding that took place in Landshut between Duke George and a Polish princess in 1475, a wedding that is restaged in the town every third year as part of a festive pageant. Rising opposite the town hall is the Residenz, built for Duke Ludwig X in the 1530s and 1540s. Ludwig's admiration for the Italian Renaissance is mirrored in the 40 rooms of this palace, which has now become the perfect setting for an art gallery (open: same hours as Burg Trausnitz – see below).

The gently curving Altstadt is closed off at one end by the Gothic church of St Martin, designed by Hans Stethaimer and built out of rose-pink brick between 1389 and 1500. Its spire, at 133m, is the tallest built of brick in the world. Five flamboyant Gothic porches pierce its walls, which are clad with memorial tablets (including a bust of Stethaimer himself and his coat of arms bearing two set squares). The lavish Gothic altar was carved in 1424, its baroque upper half dating from 1664. In front of the chancel hangs a crucifix carved by Michael Erhart in 1495. The choir stalls of around 1500 carry beautiful carvings of biblical scenes.

Above the town is Burg (Castle) Trausnitz, founded in 1204. It was later enriched by Prince William of Bavaria with a Renaissance-style gallery courtyard and a famous staircase (the Narrentreppe) frescoed in 1578 with figures from the Italian Commedia dell'Arte. As one might well expect there are splendid views over the town from the castle walls (guided tours April to September 9am–noon and 1–5pm; open: 9am–4pm for the rest of the year; admission charge). *65km northeast of Munich. Tourist office: in the Rathaus (Town Hall). Tel: 0871 23031.*

Passau's enormous cathedral rises serenely above the Donau (Danube)

PASSAU

Three rivers, the Danube, the Inn and the Ilz, all meet at Passau, which was settled by the Celts in pre-Christian times. Converted to Christianity in the mid-5th century, it was raised to the status of a bishopric by St Boniface in 739.

Alte Residenz and Neue Residenz

Both palaces sit in Residenzplatz, the Alte Residenz abutting on to Zengergasse, near the cathedral, the first built for the bishops in Renaissance style, the second in baroque. In the same square is a 13th-century pharmacy. The Neue Residenz exhibits the cathedral treasury and is also the diocesan museum.

Open: May to October and Christmas and Easter weeks 10am–4pm. Closed Sunday.

Glass Museum

Located in the house called Im Wilden Mann (the Wild Man), this displays an extensive collection of stained glass and glass vessels from all ages.

Open: daily 10am–5pm.

Stephansdom

Passau's enormous cathedral has an octagonal dome which dominates the city. Founded in the 5th century and rebuilt as a late-Gothic building from 1407, it was comprehensively rebuilt after a fire in 1680 by Carlo Lurago. Its organ, the largest church organ in the world (built in 1928 with over 17,754 pipes and 238 stops) is played each summer's day at noon and at 6pm during July and August. Below, the cathedral square is surrounded by lovely canons' houses.

Open: standard hours (see page 18).

Veste Niederhaus and Veste Oberhaus

These citadels were built respectively in the early 13th and 14th centuries to consolidate the hold of the bishops on the city. They now house the city and regional museums.

Open: March to November 9am–5pm. Closed: Monday.

Location: Passau is 150km east of Munich. Tourist office: Rathausplatz 3. Tel: 0851 955480.

WASSERBURG AM INN

This walled town sits picturesquely on a peninsula of the River Inn opposite a 15th-century castle. The town is entered by a river bridge and through a battlemented medieval gateway, built in 1374 and decorated in 1568 with a pair of hairy-faced knights. The fortified gateway across the bridge, called Brucktor, abuts on to Wasserburg's former Holy Ghost hospice (founded in 1341). This is now a shopping complex with an art gallery displaying reproductions of works ranging from Romanesque frescos to the paintings of Picasso (open: May to September 11am–5pm; rest of year 1–5pm; closed Monday).

The charming Marienplatz includes Wasserburg's 65m-high medieval watch-tower, saved from destruction by fire in 1874 by the intervention of the Virgin Mary, according to local belief. The watch-tower now serves as the belfry of a 14th-century church. Opposite stands the town's former tollhouse (the Altes Mauthaus), which was built for the Duke of Bavaria in 1497 and given a Renaissance façade with three oriel windows in 1530. In the same square is the late-Gothic Rathaus (Town Hall) built in the mid-15th century by Jörg Tünzl. Its blank windows are decorated with armorial bearings (guided tours on the hour). Opposite is the Kernhaus with a distinctive stucco façade of 1738 by Johann Baptist Zimmerman.

The town's entrancing main church, St Jakob, has a brick nave while the apse and tower are built of stone. It was begun in 1410 and completed in 1461.

Strolling through Passau

Medieval solidity: the gateway into Wasserburg am Inn

Inside little has changed since then, save for the addition of a rich Renaissance pulpit of 1639, by the brothers Martin and Michael Zürn. It is topped with a statue of the church's patron, St James the Great, carrying a pilgrim's staff.
45km east of Munich. Tourist office: in the Rathaus (Town Hall) on Marienplatz. Tel: 08071 10522.

MARIAHILF

On the far side of the River Inn is the baroque pilgrimage church of Mariahilf. Reached by 264 steps, it was built by Francesco Garbiano to enshrine a miracle working statue of the *Madonna and Child*.

Around Altötting

This circular tour of some 60km visits the Öttinger Forest and entrancing towns and villages, passing by nature reserves and along the banks of two rivers. An easy route to follow, it makes an excellent cycle tour, its gradients well within the capacity of children. *Allow 4 hours by car, 8 hours by bicycle.*

1 ALTÖTTING

Pilgrims have been coming to Altötting to seek the help of the miracle-working statue of the Black Madonna for several centuries. The statue is in the Gnadenkapelle (Chapel of Grace) on the main square, Kapellplatz. While you are here do not miss the superb Collegiate Church of St Philip and St Jakob. *Leave Altötting by way of the Alte Poststrasse, travelling southeast through the forest to Emmerting and Hohenwart.*

2 HOHENWART

This suburb, across the River Alz from Emmerting, has a little

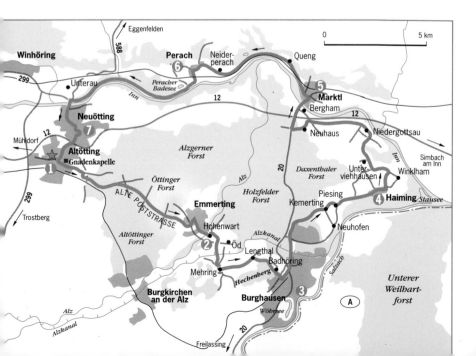

Altötting, home of the famous miracle-working Black Madonna

Gothic church dedicated to St Nikolaus, built around 1470.

Continue on to the old town of Burghausen on the River Salzach, which forms the border between Bavaria and Austria.

3 BURGHAUSEN

The town's massive fortress, Germany's largest, was begun in 1253. Part of the building is used to display pictures from the Bavarian state art collection, while elsewhere in the complex you will find a local history museum and a museum of photography.

Continue northeastwards to Haiming.

4 HAIMING

Located alongside the Stausee, Haiming has a bird reserve, a castle and the 15th-century church of St Oswald.

Continue north to follow the bank of the River Inn to Niedergottsau (with its 15th-century pilgrimage church), then cross the river to Marktl.

5 MARKTL

Set beside the River Inn, Marktl has a lakeside bathing beach, a nature reserve, a local history museum and a neo-Gothic parish church.

Continue west along the river to Perach.

6 PERACH

Here is another attractive lake, for swimming, sailing or sunbathing. The town's Romanesque parish church, Maria Himmelfahrt, was gothicised in the 15th century.

Continue west along the Inn to Neuötting.

7 NEUÖTTING

The long Marktplatz is closed at each end by a medieval gate and flanked by arcaded houses. Hans Stethaimer designed the superb brick parish church with its 78m-high spire. Begun in 1410, the fine ogival vaulting was completed in the 1620s. Dedicated to St Nikolaus, the church houses a rococo statue of the saint carrying three golden balls, a sign that he is the patron saint of pawnbrokers.

Take the road south for 3km to return to Altötting.

The Rossfeld-Ringstrasse

A spectacular drive, the Rossfeld Ring Road is a superb piece of 1930s mountain engineering on which you can drive, or take a bus, from Oberau to Obersalzberg (or, if you prefer, the other way round). The Ringstrasse is 16.4km long, has sharp bends and steep gradients. Often used for motor rallies and even displays of vintage cars, it reaches a height of 1,600m. *Allow 1 hour.*

From Berchtesgaden, follow the signs indicating Rossfeld and Rossfeldstrasse. Motorists must pay a toll to use the road.

The Ringstrasse passes through a region frequented alike by skiers and by sunbathers. Even in winter, when thick snow covers the Alps through which the road passes, visitors are to be seen seated in deckchairs facing the sun. Along the road there

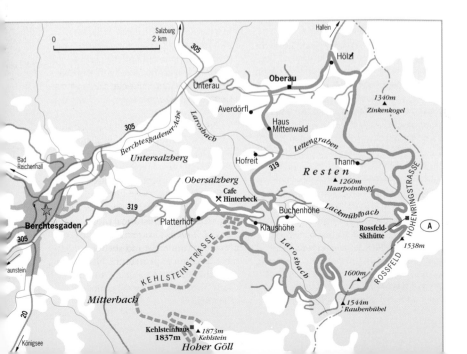

are numerous parking spaces. From these you can often see hang-gliders floating by, virtually at eye-level. Snow-clad crags and deep clefts in the rocks appear as you drive. Eventually you will be able to see Bavaria on one side, Austria on the other. You will also see several awesome Alpine peaks. The closest to the Ringstrasse is the Hoher Göll, whose peak reaches 2,522m. Further away, to the southwest, you can see the Watzmann (2,713m). To the east, across the Austrian border, are two mountain ranges – the Tennengebirge and, in the distance, the Dachstein-gebirge whose highest point is 2,996m above sea level.

Continue to Hintereck, which is the starting point for a visit to the Kehlstein, the once notorious Eagle's Nest. Private cars are no longer allowed along the road from Hintereck to Kehlstein. From the end of May to October access is via a regular bus service which picks up visitors at Hintereck. The last buses leave about 1pm. It is also possible to walk to Kehlstein along a 6.5km-long footpath.

Formidable cliffs and snow-clad crags contrast with mountain meadows

Martin Bormann, the Nazi politician, conceived the idea of presenting Adolf Hitler with the Kehlsteinhaus, perched 1,837m high on a spur of the Hoher Göll above Obersalzberg, for his 50th birthday. Within 13 months a road had been blasted from Obersalzberg up to Kehlstein. The plan was to entertain foreign diplomats here, but to Bormann's chagrin Hitler never liked the spot and rarely came. Instead he preferred to entertain such guests as the British Prime Minister Neville Chamberlain and the French statesman and collaborator Pierre Laval at the chalet in Obersalzberg that he had been renting since 1925. Although the Allies wished to destroy

the Kehlsteinhaus after World War II, the Bürgermeister of Berchtesgaden persuaded them to change their minds. The Eagle's Nest thus became a restaurant from which there are superb views. Its walls, a metre thick, reveal the anxieties of the Hitler régime, and its architecture is an historical monument of that era. Traces also remain of the network of underground shelters which were designed to protect the Nazi leaders (access to these can be gained from the Hotel Türken near the car park in Obersalzberg).

The Königssee

The green waters of the Königssee, the Bavarians claim, are the cleanest in Germany and since 1978 the lake and its surroundings have been designated as the Berchtesgaden National Park. Stretching for 8km, and 2km at its widest, the Königssee is over 190m deep and the surrounding cliffs fall almost sheer to the bottom of the lake. Königssee is also surrounded by breathtakingly beautiful mountains, the highest of which is the Watzmann. Throughout the seasons its shores present an ever-changing range of colours, with thick snow in winter, startlingly powerful waterfalls in spring and green vegetation in summer changing to autumnal hues as the months pass. *Allow 1¼ hours for the ferry trip.*

To reach the lake you can take a bus from Berchtesgaden's railway station to the village of Königssee. From there, 21 electrically powered boats take passengers soundlessly across the lake to St Bartholomä.

1 THE FERRY JOURNEY

At various points the lakeside cliffs give off a resounding echo; the crew may well stop the boat while one of their number blows a trumpet fanfare – everyone waits in silence until the notes are tossed back by the cliffs (the crew will then take a collection). The journey then continues to Schönau am Königssee, a village halfway down the western shore of the lake that is usually named after its baroque church of St Bartholomä.

2 ST BARTHOLOMÄ

One tower of the church is onion-domed, while the second has a round

The clear waters of Königssee

Boat houses, inns and balconied chalets cluster round Königssee's shores

cap with a jaunty peak. The roof also has three little domes. The church dates back to 1134 and it was a favourite pilgrimage spot for Bavarians (pilgrims still come on 24 August). The priors who once ruled Berchtesgaden had a hunting lodge here, which is now a restaurant serving fish caught in the lake. When the Berchtesgaden region became Bavarian in 1810 (previously it had been part of Austria) this became a favourite spot of the royal family who vigorously dedicated themselves to hunting and fishing. Shades of the long-dead great haunt this exquisite spot. Here, for example, the royal architect Karl Friedrich Schinkel and the Romantic artist Caspar David Friedrich found rest and inspiration.

3 EXCURSION TO THE WATZMANN

Intrepid walkers can join an organised party for the one-hour trek to the east face of the mighty Watzmann.

You can break your journey at St Bartholomä before resuming your ferry journey. A further half-hour sail from St Bartholomä will bring you to Salet. From here a 15-minute walk on a clearly signposted track brings you to the Obersee.

4 OBERSEE

The waters of this smaller and wilder-looking lake reflect the Hagen mountain range, Austria. On the left the Röthbach waterfall tumbles 400m into the lake. The Obersee is the starting point for numerous walks and hikes of varying difficulty, the most pleasant taking you around the lake to the Alpine region known as Fischunkel Alm in 45 minutes.

BOAT TRIPS

In summer the boats depart from Königssee every 15 minutes, starting at 7.15am. In spring and autumn trips begin at 8.15am and the boats leave every 20 minutes. In winter they start at 9.45am, leaving every 45 minutes. Make sure you check the times of the last boat back.

For further information contact: Staatliche Schiffahrt Königssee, Seestrasse 55, 8240 Schönau am Königssee (tel: 08652 4026).

The Alpenstrasse

The Alpine Road (Deutsche Alpenstrasse)
stretches from Lindau on the Bodensee (Lake
Constance) to Berchtesgaden, a distance of nearly
300km. Since this scenic route is too far to
explore comfortably in one day, try touring just
the easternmost part, starting at Grassau and
driving along the B305 to Ramsau, just outside
Berchtesgaden, a distance of 91km, made exciting by
hairpin bends and occasional 15 per cent gradients.

*Start at Grassau, reached from Munich by taking the A8 autobahn
southeast for about 78km, then the B305 road south for 13km.*

1 GRASSAU
This holiday and health resort is dominated by the 1,586m-
high Hochplatte and boasts a late-Gothic parish church with
a Romanesque tower.
Drive 3km southeast along the B305 to Marquartstein.

2 MARQUARTSTEIN
The composer Richard Strauss lived in Bursagstrasse where he
composed his *Salome* and his *Feuersnot*. Alongside the town's
parish church is a signpost directing visitors to a nature park
and a children's fairy-tale garden.
*Running in a southerly direction, the B305 now winds for 17km to
Reit im Winkl.*

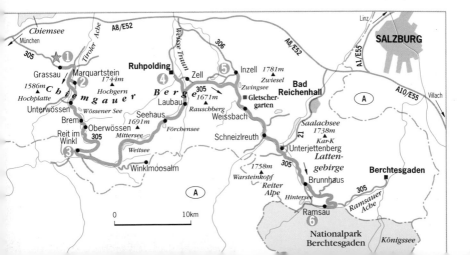

3 REIT IM WINKL

This Alpine holiday resort, on the
Austrian border, flourishes in summer as
well as in winter as ski lifts take visitors
up to peaks that offer exhilarating
panoramas.
*Drive 24km northeast, through countryside
dotted with lakes, to Ruhpolding.*

4 RUHPOLDING

In spite of its 7,000 inhabitants,
Ruhpolding nonetheless preserves the
charm of an Alpine village. The castle,
built in 1597, houses a local history
museum and there is a colourful 1930s
Rathaus (Town Hall). The parish church
of St George is one of the prettiest in the
whole region, with a Romanesque façade
and a mid-18th-century nave. The glory
of the church is the Ruhpolding
Madonna. Carved out of wood around
1230, she sits on the altar at the right-
hand side of the apse. Ruhpolding's
17th-century cemetery chapel is also
fascinating, with historic gravestones
decorating the walls both inside and out.
The town also has a miniature park, with
models of celebrated German buildings.
Drive another 13km east to find Inzell.

5 INZELL

See page 80.
*Next drive 34km southeast along the B305
to Ramsau.*

6 RAMSAU

This health and winter sports resort has
a charming baroque pilgrimage church
(Maria Kunterweg) which dates from
1733. The town's parish church was
founded in the early 16th century and is
like a scene from a Christmas card.
Inside, old family names are set into
personal pews. Gothic statues of Christ
and the Apostles enhance the organ loft.

Charming details arrest the eye in the
town of Ruhpolding

The Hintersee lake, 4km westwards, is
popular with anglers, swimmers and
sailing enthusiasts.

Grassau's church, with its onion-domed tower,
first stop on the Alpenstrasse

Around Inzell

This spectacular Alpine walk through beech-woods, pastures and stony mountain peaks is very demanding and should only be undertaken in summer and with proper walking shoes. The route is marked on the *Wanderkarte* map which is available from the tourist office in Inzell.
Allow 8 hours.

1 INZELL

Inzell is a delightful village, set in a valley with fine views of the mountains. The parish church of St Michael was founded by Archbishop Albrecht II of Salzburg in 1190. Most of this building was burned down in 1724, leaving only the Romanesque belfry, which supports a baroque onion dome. The new nave, begun three years after the fire, is beautifully decorated and has a splendid organ loft. Opposite is the

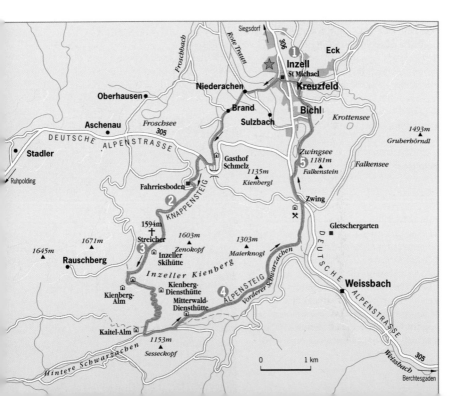

Rathaus, and there are plenty of good local inns, including the early-16th-century Gasthof zur Post.

Passing the parish church and graveyard, take the road to Niederachen, walking through Brand to reach the Gasthof Schmelz. Turn right at the Gasthof, crossing the main road, and look for a narrow path that climbs steeply through mountain woods to the chapel of Fahrriesboden. Turn left here to walk for some 200m until you reach a steep track (the Knappensteig) running off to the right.

2 THE KNAPPENSTEIG

The Knappensteig brings you to the entrance of several tunnels belonging to a disued mine.

Next it crosses scree slopes and then makes its way through pine trees. This is where the route becomes extremely steep. You will eventually reach a saddle offering views of the mountains to the south. To the right a cross crowns the nearest peak.

3 MOUNTAIN PEAKS

The view from the cross takes in such peaks as the Watzmann, the Hochkalter, the Hochheissspitze and the Reiter Alpe. Close by is the Inzeller Skihütte, the ski-hut of the Inzell sports club.

From the mountain cross the route now runs past the ski-hut to Kienberg-Alm, where you turn left to reach the Kienberg hunting lodge (the Kienberg Diensthütte). Dizzily twisting southwards, the Alpine road will now take you to Kaitel-Alm.

4 ALPENSTEIG

At Kaitel-Alm turn sharply left to hike to the Alpensteig (Alpine Track) which you follow until it eventually arrives at Zwing. Here you can take the opportunity for a break in the Café Zwing.

Inzell, base for this demanding walk

5 ZWINGSEE

Turn north to walk through woods and alongside the German Alpine Road (Deutsche Alpenstrasse) as far as the Zwingsee. The route runs around the right-hand side of the lake. At the far side of the lake keep walking north-easterly and then turn northwards, hiking through meadows lying at the foot of the Falkenstein range, to reach Bichl.

Further north is Kreuzfeld, where you turn left at the Gasthaus Falkenstein and walk on under the Bundesstrasse back to Inzell.

Watzmann, Germany's second highest peak

Southwest Bavaria

AUGSBURG

The name of Augsburg, a city cooled by elaborate 16th-century fountains, indicates its antiquity, for the legions of the Roman Emperor Augustus founded a camp here where the Rivers Lech and Wertach meet. In the Middle Ages Augsburg became a city of wealthy bankers, in particular the Fugger family. Great artists, including Hans Holbein the Elder and his son Hans Holbein the Younger, lived and worked here. For a walk round the town, see page 96.

Domkirche (Cathedral)

Founded in 823, the oldest part of Augsburg's cathedral is the crypt. Inside there are four paintings by Hans Holbein the Elder and five stained-glass windows (in the south clerestory) dating from the 12th century and the oldest in Germany. On the south side are mid-14th-century bronze doors decorated with 35 reliefs depicting scenes from the Old Testament. *Frauentorstrasse. Open: standard hours (see page 18).*

Fuggerei

These almshouses were founded in 1516 by Jakob Fugger 'the Rich'. *Mittler Gasse 13. Open: March to 31 October, daily 9am–6pm; November and December, Saturdays and Sundays only.*

Heiligkreuzkirche

Martin Luther often preached in this lovely Renaissance church. *Heiligkreuzstrasse. Open: standard hours (see page 18).*

Rathausplatz

The city's main square centres on the Augustus fountain, created by Hubert Gerhard in 1594 to celebrate the 1,600th anniversary of the founding of the city. It features a statue of the Emperor Augustus and symbols of the four rivers of the region. To one side of the square is Elias Holl's magnificent Renaissance town hall completed in 1620. Its Golden Hall has a superb coffered ceiling and wall paintings (open: daily 10am–6pm).

The Perlachturm, rising alongside Peterkirche, offers fine views from the

Augsburg is cooled by many fountains

ZOO

Augsburg Zoo is set in 22 hectares of parkland on the borders of the Siebentisch forest and features over 2,000 animals and birds from all over the world.
Open: daily 8.30am–6.30pm; to 5pm in winter. Tel: 0821 555031. Bus 32 from Augsburg Central Station to Königsbrunn.

AUGSBURG

top (open: 1 April to 30 September, daily 10am–6pm; October, 10am–4pm).

St Ulrich und St Afra

Founded in 1474, this late-Gothic basilica is crammed with Renaissance and baroque works of art.
Maximilianstrasse. Open: standard hours (see page 18).

Schaezlerpalais

The palace displays a collection of German baroque and rococo paintings.
Maximilianstrasse 46. Open: Wednesday to Sunday 10am–5pm, to 4pm October to April.

Location. Augsburg is 50km west of Munich. Tourist office: Verkehrsverein, Bahnhofstrasse 7. Tel: 0821 5020 70.

ETTAL

In 1327, Ludwig the Bavarian, Duke of Bavaria and Holy Roman Emperor, made a pilgrimage to Rome where he bought a statue of the Virgin Mary. On the return journey the emperor's horse stopped at Ettal (so the legend runs) and genuflected to the statue. This inspired Ludwig to found a splendid Benedictine monastery here with an unusual 12-sided abbey church, modelled on the Church of the Holy Sepulchre in Jerusalem.

Most of the old abbey (though not the statue of the Virgin Mary) was destroyed in a fire of 1744. In rebuilding the church, the Italian Enrico Zuccalli, assisted by the Bavarian Franz Xavier Schmuzer, created one of Bavaria's finest rococo buildings. His church, which retains the 12-sided pattern of its predecessor, is surmounted by a dome designed by Schmuzer and the interior is frescoed with over 400 figures glorifying the Benedictine order of monks. The high altar enshrines the statue brought by Ludwig the Bavarian from Rome, and Johann Baptist Zimmermann contributed an inspired pink and white rococo organ loft and organ case.

70km south of Munich, 6km southeast of Oberammergau. Tourist office: Ammergauer Strasse 8. Tel: 08822 3534.

FÜSSEN

Füssen grew up around an 8th-century monastery founded to enshrine the bones of St Mang (or Magnus). The original abbey has, for the most part, been superseded by 18th-century baroque buildings created by Johann Jakob Herkomer (though the crypt remains 11th-century). Today it houses the local history museum (open: summer, Tuesday to Sunday 11am–4pm; winter 2–4pm).

Close by, and picturesquely set on a hill, is the Hohenschloss. This was built in 1322 for the Prince-Bishop of

Ettal's 12-sided abbey church

SOUTHWEST BAVARIA

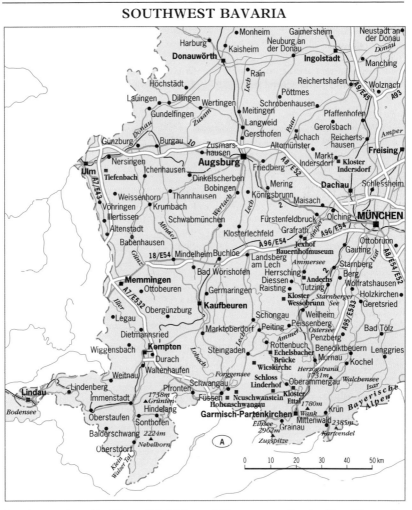

Augsburg, enlarged by Bishop Friedrich von Zollern around 1500 and extended again in the 19th century for King Max I. The Gothic chapel has a fine *Coronation of the Virgin*, painted around 1500. The east wing, added in the early 14th century, encompasses the Knights' Hall with its 16th-century coffered ceiling. The north wing displays paintings from the Bavarian national collection (open: summer, Tuesday to Sunday 11am–4pm; winter 2–4pm).

120km southwest of Munich. Tourist office: Kaiser-Maximilian Platz 1. Tel: 08362 7077.

The twin towns of Garmisch and Partenkirchen lie beneath Zugspitze's peaks

GARMISCH-PARTENKIRCHEN

The twin towns of Garmisch and Partenkirchen together form one of Germany's most popular resorts, beautifully sited at the foot of the Alps. The 1936 winter Olympics were held here and the 1978 world skiing championships. As a result the town has become a premier wintersports centre, with an Olympic ski-jump and ice stadium. Garmisch-Partenkirchen also remains a haven for hikers in summer.

Several of the nearby peaks are accessible by cable car or rack railway, including Germany's highest mountain Zugspitze (2,962m), Wank (1,780m) and Eckbauer (1,237m). Close to the town is the beautiful Partnachklamm gorge, dubbed one of 'the Wonders of the World'. It is reached on foot or by means of a horse and carriage from the Olympic ice stadium along a 2km road

(cars are banned). A path runs through the gorge which is remarkably narrow and deep, with a number of unusual rock formations. Another popular sight is the tiny Lake Badersee, in the little village of Grainau, just west of Garmisch-Partenkirchen. Boats can be hired here that will take you to see the statue of the water nymph, Nixe, placed at the bottom of the lake by King Ludwig II.
120km southwest of Munich. Tourist office: Schnitzschulstrasse 19. Tel: 08821 1800.

IMMENSTADT

Immenstadt is an enticing little Alpine town and a fine centre for skiing and hiking (with marked routes). It is conveniently close to the Grosser Alpsee lake which in summer is used for water sports. The ambience of the spot is enhanced by the surrounding mountains, dominated by the Grünten (1,738m).
149km southwest of Munich, 55km east of Lindau. Tourist office: in the Rathaus on Marienplatz. Tel: 08323 914176.

KEMPTEN

Kempten is a busy commercial town with a number of good museums devoted to archaeology and local history (all open: Tuesday to Sunday 10am–4pm). They include the Alpenmuseum (Alpine Museum) and the Zumsteinhaus, a fine classical building of 1802 used to display archaeological finds from the site of the original Roman town of *Cambodunum*; the latter stands at the centre of an archaeological park to the east of town, across the River Iller (open: May to September, Tuesday to Sunday 10am–5pm; to 4.30pm November to April, but closed January and February).
124km southwest of Munich. Tourist office: Rathausplatz 24. Tel: 0831 252 5237.

KLEIN WALSER TAL

This exquisite valley is overlooked by the bizarrely shaped rocks of the Widderstein (which rises to 2,533m) and such dramatic peaks as the Grünhorn (2,039m) and the Hoher Ifen (2,230m). Oddly enough the valley belongs to Austria but can only be entered from Bavaria (you need a passport to cross the frontier). In consequence its currency is German, though its vehicles bear Austrian number plates.

This is a paradise for wintersports fanatics, and the valley's three major towns are all entrancing. The facilities at Riezlern include a casino and dance-cafés. At Hirschegg there is a pleasant theatre, swimming pools, sauna, golf and bowling courses and tennis courts. Mittelberg has a baroque church and some of the 18th-century houses have painted façades. There is also a pleasant public garden, the Kurpark in Riezlern.
190km southwest of Munich, 55km south of Kempten. Tourist office: Im Walserhaus, Hirschegg. Tel: 08329 51140.

Sunshine on the flowerbeds and buildings in Kempten

LANDSBERG AM LECH

If you are visiting this lovely hillside town you can follow the well-signposted town walk, the Stadtrundgang, which will take you down characterful alleys to the town's 15th-century walls, from where there are good views of the River Lech. A free walk map can be collected from the tourist office in the main square, Hauptplatz. Here, too, you can see the superb Rathaus (Town Hall) with its rich stucco façade designed by one of Bavaria's finest architects, Domenikus Zimmermann, who served as the town's Bürgermeister (Mayor) between 1759 and 1764. Also worth seeing is the 16th-century stained glass in the choir of the Maria Himmelfahrt church.

54km west of Munich. Tourist office: Hauptplatz 1. Tel: 08191 128246.

LINDAU

Lindau sits on an island at the east end of the Bodensee, better known as Lake Constance, the second largest of the Alpine lakes (after Lake Geneva). Lindau's harbour is home to a fleet of boats that carry visitors round the 65km-long lake, which forms the border between Bavaria and Austria. The harbour is guarded by a statue of the heraldic Lion of Bavaria and two lighthouses – one dating from the 13th century and once part of the city's fortifications, the other from 1865.

The town itself has delightful traffic-free lakeside promenades while Alstadt is lined by attractive medieval and baroque houses. At St Peter's Church you can see the only frescos to have survived by Hans Holbein the Elder, dating from the 1480s.

190km southwest of Munich. Tourist office: Bahnhofplatz. Tel: 08382 260030.

LINDERHOF

Of the three castles built by King Ludwig II (see page 94) Linderhof is the most endearing because of its lovely formal gardens and its woodland setting. Ludwig intended the castle as a 'new Versailles' but the original lavish scheme was never realised. Instead this fine rococo villa was built, with its Hall of Mirrors and its extraordinary dining table, designed to be lowered to the kitchen below and hoisted back up laden with dishes full of food. In the garden is the Venus Grotto (closed in winter), an artificial cave that Wagner used to stage his opera, *Tannhäuser*. Germany's first ever electric lighting scheme was devised to illuminate the cave's waterfall and lake.

100km southwest of Munich, 20km west of Oberammergau. Open: daily 9am–12.15pm and 12.45–5.30pm in summer, to 4pm in winter. Admission charge.

OBERAMMERGAU

Home of Germany's most celebrated Passion Play (see pages 90–1), Oberammergau is also a typically beautiful Alpine village. That beauty is enhanced by the work of the 18th-century local artist Franz Joseph Zwinck, who developed to perfection the art of *trompe l'oeil* painting and decorated several houses in the town with scenes giving the illusion of three-dimensional columned halls and swirling steps. Many shops in the town sell locally carved wooden figures, mostly on religious themes, and you can see a display of historic Christmas cribs in the local history museum on Dorfstrasse (open: 15 May to 15 October, 2–6pm; rest of year Saturdays only; closed: Monday).

You can also visit the Passions theater (open: May to October, 9.30am–noon, 1–4pm; November to April, 10am–noon, 1–4pm). This is a severely functional building but the acoustics are perfect. Backstage is an informative exhibition of costumes and props used in the Passion Play.

More spectacular is the parish church of St Peter and St Paul, by the rococo architect Joseph Schmuzer. He designed the double organ loft and painted the third (*trompe l'oeil*) loft above it. In the great dome Matthäus Günther painted the martyrdoms of St Peter and St Paul and their entry into the heavenly Jerusalem. Franz Xavier Schmädl

sculpted the pulpit and the magnificent high altar with its drapery, up and down which a host of cherubs fly.

The cemetery contains the graves of Alois Daisenberger, the pastor to whom Oberammergau owes the present form of its Passion Play, and Rochus Dedler, who composed its music.

100km southwest of Munich. Tourist office: Eugen-Papst-Strasse 9a. Tel: 08822 1021.

The gorgeous Hall of Mirrors at Linderhof Castle, one of several lavish rooms

THE OBERAMMERGAU

THE PLAGUE

Although plagues were endemic in 17th-century Bavaria, the Thirty Years' War made them even more frequent, with marauding armies spreading disease. The war was in its fourteenth year when the plague reached Oberammergau in 1632, brought by an infected man from nearby Eschenlohe who crept into the village at night, evading the guards set to keep strangers out. By the end of the year the disease he brought had killed 84 villagers.

THE VOW

The following July all those who were still able to walk processed to the parish church and solemnly vowed that if God

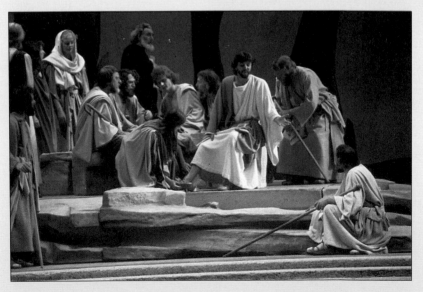

PASSION PLAY

Initially the citizens of Oberammergau borrowed a play written earlier by the monks of Augsburg. Today the play is essentially that written by Oberammergau's mid-19th-century parish priest, Alois Daisenberger. The play is accompanied by the baroque music composed for earlier performances by Rochus Dedler (born in Oberammergau in 1799). Another feature is the 'Living Tableaux' – episodes from the Old Testament in which the scene, though crowded with actors, is motionless, an event frozen in time.

TODAY

As always, the Passion Play is performed solely by those born in the village and competition for the major parts is very keen. Nowadays so many visitors come to see the play that each of the main roles is given to two actors who perform on alternate days throughout the Passion Play season. The play, which takes all day to perform, involves a cast of 1,700 and is seen by over half a million people during the 100-day season.

lifted the plague, they would perform a Passion Play every 10 years, recounting the events of Holy Week from Christ's triumphant entry into Jerusalem on Palm Sunday to the Crucifixion and subsequent Resurrection. From that moment no other villager died of the disease. So 1634 saw the first performance of the Passion Play, 1644 the second. As time passed the play began to be performed at the turn of each decade, so that the most recent performances took place in 1990.

Aspects of Oberammergau

OTTOBEUREN

Ottobeuren is the site of one of Germany's largest churches, a mighty baroque building with a nave 90m long. It was built to serve the town's Benedictine abbey, originally founded in 764, which prospered under the patronage of the Holy Roman Emperor, Charlemagne. The church was rebuilt in 1737 by Johann Michael Fischer and several other major artists contributed to the light and airy cathedral-like interior with its fine frescos and splendid organ. Near to Ottobeuren is the large town of Memmingen, with its attractive medieval centre and the splendid Gothic spire of St Martinskirche.

120km west of Munich. Tourist office: Marktplatz 14, Ottobeuren. Tel: 08332 921950.

SCHWANGAU

Schwangau is a quite charming rustic village, famous principally as a base for visiting the splendid royal castles of Hohenschwangau and Neuschwanstein. Both castles enjoy a spectacular setting against the backdrop of Alpine crags, but both can also be very crowded.

Early morning mist in Schwangau

Hohenschwangau

Hohenschwangau, the lower and older of the two castles, rises on the spot where a stronghold of the Knights of the Swan stood from the 12th century until Napoleon Bonaparte demolished it. In 1832 the future King Max II commissioned the theatre architect Dominik Quaglio to re-create a medieval dream castle here. After Quaglio's death in 1837, Joseph Daniel Ohlmüller and G F Ziebland finished the work.

The 14 rooms that are open to visitors glorify the Wittelsbach dynasty. Statues of Emperor Ludwig the Bavarian and Elector Maximilian I flank the entrance. The deeds of Germany's medieval heroes are portrayed in frescos commissioned from Moritz von Schwind and Wilhelm Lindenschmidt. Here, too, are portraits of Charlemagne and Martin Luther. Richard Wagner (see page 116) often stayed at Hohenschwangau, and his opera *Lohengrin* inspired the decoration of the Hall of the Knights of the Swan: here the seats and the huge silver chandelier have swan motifs and the centrepiece is another silver swan, a wedding present from the citizens of Munich to Maximilian.

Hohenschwangau is filled with oddities, none more so than the Queen's Bedroom, which is in the Turkish style (a consequence of Maximilian's visit to Turkey in 1833) and furnished with settees given by Sultan Muhammed II. Another curiosity is the bedroom of Maximilian's son, the future Ludwig II, which is decorated with stars that could be lit up dramatically in the evening when the prince retired for the night.

Neuschwanstein

Neuschwanstein is the splendid creation of King Ludwig II. Though unfinished at

A pensive monarch considers the deeds of German heroes at Hohenschwangau

the time of his mysterious death (only 15 out of a projected 65 rooms were built), it remains one of the world's most stunningly romantic fairy-tale castles. Part of a mountain peak was blasted away to provide it with a solid base, and to reach the castle involves a hard uphill climb – alternatively you can take a bus, or a more romantic horse-drawn carriage from the car park.

Ludwig commissioned the architects Eduard Riedl, Georg Dollmann and Julius Hofmann to create this masterpiece of fantasy and pseudo-medievalism. Throughout there are references to the unreal world of Wagner's operas. The decoration of the entrance hall was inspired by the *Nibelungen* cycle; the dining room and the king's study are painted with scenes from *Tannhäuser*; Ludwig's living room

and bedroom display scenes from *Tristan and Isolde*; the décor of the Sängersaal (Singers' Hall) was inspired by *Parsifal*, and the upper courtyard is based on an 1867 set designed for *Lohengrin*.

Neuschwanstein displays remarkable feats of engineering and artistry, with its winding staircases, columns sculpted like palm trees and its Byzantine throne room with a golden chandelier weighing 900kg and a marble floor incorporating over 2.5 million pieces. Equally enthralling are the vistas of the Bavarian Alps and of nearby lakes that reveal themselves through the windows as you explore the castle. *120km southwest of Munich. Open: guided tours of both castles take place daily in summer 9am–5.30pm and in winter 10am–4pm. Admission charge. Tourist office: Münchenerstrasse 2, Schwangau. Tel: 08362 81051.*

LUDWIG – THE

In August 1845 a long-awaited heir to the Bavarian throne was born. Christened Ludwig, he spent most of his childhood in romantic isolation at Hohenschwangau (see page 92) where, at the age of 16, he became enraptured by the music of Richard Wagner (see page 116).

In 1864 he was crowned King Ludwig II. If his friendship with Wagner brought him enemies, his foreign policy made him even more detested, for he supported his ministers in a war against Prussia which ended in ignominious defeat after only three weeks, and Bavaria was forced to pay the Prussians 50 million marks in gold as a penalty. When the Franco-Prussian War of 1870 broke out, Ludwig and his ministers made the wiser decision to side with Prussia.

In the meantime he spent lavish sums building his dream castles: Schloss Herrenchiemsee (see page 67), Schloss Neuschwanstein (page 92) and Schloss Linderhof (page 88). All three are replete with references to two of Ludwig's idols, Richard Wagner and the French King Louis XIV.

Left and top left: the dining room and ceiling detail at Schloss Linderhof

FAIRY TALE KING

Herrenchiemsee is virtually a replica of Versailles, the palace of Louis XIV, while the French king's motto *Nec pluribus impar* is embossed on the ceilings at Linderhof and there are statues of Louis XIV in the entrance hall and the garden. Linderhof also exhibits examples of Ludwig's eccentric lifestyle: the table in the dining room could be cranked up to Ludwig so that he could eat alone without ever seeing his servants.

Ludwig spent his own private fortune on his castles and got the state deeply into debt. His alarmed ministers persuaded doctors to declare the king insane, forcing him to abdicate and to submit to house arrest at Schloss Berg, a castle beside the Starnberg Lake. On Whitsunday 1886 his body, along with that of his physician Dr von Gudden, were discovered mysteriously drowned in the lake. To this day it remains a mystery whether Ludwig died accidentally or deliberately – whether he committed suicide or was murdered.

Equally the world remains divided as to whether Ludwig was a misunderstood genius or simply mad. In any event, the castles he once built at great cost have now repaid the investment many times over in the revenue from the millions of visitors who come to see them every year.

Top right and left: the concert hall and the King's study, Schloss Neuschwanstein

Würzburg
BAVARIA

Augsburg München ■ ·Altötting

·Berchtesgaden

Augsburg

This walk shows you the main sights of Augsburg, Bavaria's oldest city, founded in the reign of Augustus, the first Roman emperor, in the 1st century BC (see map on page 83 for the route). *Allow 2 hours.*

Begin at the Heiligkreuzkirche.

1 HEILIGKREUZKIRCHE

Built by Johann Jakob Krauss in 1653, this church served the Augustinian monastery where Martin Luther used to stay and it houses numerous mementoes of the Reformation (including a portrait of Luther and his ally, Philipp Melanchthon, and paintings of 1730 by Johann August Corvinus depicting scenes from Luther's life). The church houses many other fine

paintings, including Tintoretto's entrancing depiction of *The Baptism of Christ*, and an *Assumption* on the high altar by Peter Paul Rubens. In Heiligkreuzstrasse, Kaiser Maximilian I lived at No 4, a modest house for an emperor, from 1504 to 1519.

From the east end of the church follow Jesuitengasse, passing (on your left) the Kleiner Goldener Saal, a baroque concert hall of 1765. Turn right along Frauentorstrasse to reach the Domkirche (cathedral – see page 82). From here take Hoher Weg and Karolinenstrasse to Rathausplatz.

2 RATHAUSPLATZ

The town-hall square has a fine late-16th-century fountain with statues representing the Emperor Augustus and four of the region's rivers. Near by, the Perlachturm began life as an 11th-century watch-tower but was raised to more than 70m in height by Elias Holl in 1616. It houses a 35-bell glockenspiel which chimes daily at noon. Behind the

Quiet morning in Augsburg

Perlachturm rises the 12th-century Romanesque Peterskirche, the Church of St Peter. Behind the Rathaus (see page 82), in Elias-Holl-Platz, is Die Ecke, an inn founded in 1492.

With your back to the Rathaus, cross Rathausplatz to the traffic-free shopping area of St Anna, named after a former Carmelite church.

3 ST-ANNA-KIRCHE

This Gothic church, founded in 1321, gave shelter to Luther in 1518 after whom the Lutherhof cloister of 1521 is named. Its highlights are the Goldsmith's chapel, built in the 1420s and still preserving 15th-century wall paintings, and the Renaissance funeral chapel which Hans Burkmaier created for the Fuggers between 1508 and 1519.

Retrace your steps to Maximilianstrasse.

4 MAXIMILIANSTRASSE

Cobbled Maximilianstrasse threads through the heart of the St Anna district, following the course of the Roman Via Claudia. It is one of the finest (and certainly one of the longest surviving) medieval streets in Europe.

5 STADTPALAST DER FUGGER

At Maximilianstrasse 36 you will find the Fugger Palace, built between 1512 and 1515 for Jakob Fugger. It incorporates a lovely arcaded interior, frescoed by Hans Burkmaier, and Elias Holl's Zeughaus (Arsenal), built in 1607 and his first job as Augsburg's city architect.

Further south is the fine Herkulesbrunnen (Hercules Fountain) made between 1596 and 1602. Opposite stands the most sumptuous baroque building in the city, the Schaezlerpalais (see page 83). Beyond it is the former St Catherine's convent of 1516, today the Staatsgalerie (City Art Gallery).

6 STAATSGALERIE

The gallery displays works by several great artists, including Hans Holbein the Elder, Lukas Cranach the Elder, Canaletto, Veronese and Tiepolo (open: Tuesday to Saturday 10am–5pm, closing at 4pm from October to April). At Maximilianstrasse 83, the Welser Küche has a medieval cellar which serves food derived from a 16th-century cookery book written by Philippine Welser, wife of the Habsburg Archduke Ferdinand.

The street continues to Ulrichsplatz and the basilica of St Ulrich und St Afra.

7 ST ULRICH UND ST AFRA

Built on the site of a Roman temple, this church was founded by Kaiser Maximilian I in 1474 and built by Burkhardt Engelberg between 1476 and 1500 (see page 83). It shelters many Fugger family tombs, as well as the relics of both its patron saints. St Ulrich lies in a rococo tomb. The asymmetrical tower of the basilica was topped with an onion dome around 1600 and this set the fashion that is now typical of Bavarian church architecture.

Elias Holl's magnificent Renaissance Rathaus in Rathausplatz

Central Bavaria

ANSBACH

Set amidst the forests of the Rezat valley, Ansbach is the venue of an international Bach festival held every odd-numbered year at the end of July.

Markgrafenschloss

Ansbach was ruled by the Margraves of Brandenburg-Ansbach, for whom this splendid palace was built in the first half of the 18th century. Inside you will find a double-storeyed Great Hall, exuberantly frescoed by Christian Carlone, and a hall of mirrors containing some superb porcelain figures. The castle is surrounded by parkland containing stately avenues of lime trees laid out some 250 years ago. There is also a fine baroque orangery built in 1736. In the garden there is a memorial to the so-called 'wolf-boy', Kaspar Hauser, a foundling discovered wandering in Nuremberg in 1828, who was murdered here in mysterious circumstances.

CENTRAL BAVARIA

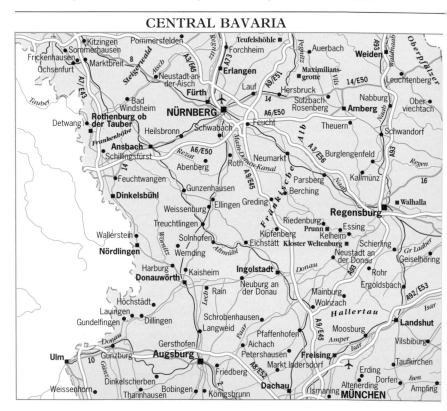

Open: Tuesday to Sunday, summer
9am–noon, 2–5pm; winter 10am–noon,
2–4pm. Admission charge.

St Gumbert

Triple-towered St Gumbert shelters the
tombs of 11 Knights of the Swan (an
order founded by Elector Friedrich II of
Brandenburg in 1440). The altar of the
Order of the Swan was carved by Martin
Wohlgemut or his pupils in 1484. The
church has a Romanesque crypt and a
funeral vault with 25 tombs of the
Margraves and their relatives.
Open: standard hours (see page 18).

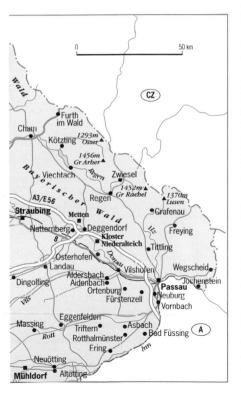

Location: Ansbach is 165km northwest of
Munich, 55km southwest of Nürnberg.
Tourist office: in the Stadthaus. Tel: 0981
51243.

DINKELSBÜHL

Dinkelsbühl is a gem of a town on the
Romantische Strasse (the Romantic
Road – see page 108) set within a ring of
picturesque walls around which you can
stroll, just as the town's nightwatchman
does every evening.

Martin Luther Strasse, the town's
main street, leads to Marktplatz with the
15th-century parish church of St George.
This is one of Bavaria's grandest
churches, with a resplendent late-Gothic
fan vault soaring high above the nave.
*150km northwest of Munich, 83km
southwest of Nürnberg. Tourist office:
Marktplatz. Tel: 09851 90240.*

DONAUWÖRTH

Beautifully situated at the point where
the River Wörnitz joins the Danube, this
town has two medieval gateways and
several elegant streets, the finest of which
is the Reichsstrasse. Dominating
Reichstrasse is the huge tower of the
Church of the Assumption. The mid-
15th-century church has frescos and
stained-glass windows of the same date,
and a stone tabernacle carved around
1600. Deutschordenshaus, formerly a
commandery of the Teutonic Knights,
was built at the end of the 18th century.
It is now a museum devoted to the
composer Werner Egk, who died in
1983. Near by is the Fuggerhaus, a
patrician home built in 1539 by Anton
Fugger at the corner of Heilig-Kreuz-
Strasse and Pflegerstrasse.
*90km northwest of Munich, 37km north of
Augsburg. Tourist office: in the Rathaus.
Tel: 0906 789145.*

EICHSTÄTT

The great cathedral church in Eichstätt was founded by the missionary St Willibald in AD740. Built in a mixture of

Massive towers in Ingolstadt recall the town's military role as a Danube garrison

The cathedral city of Eichstätt

Romanesque, Gothic and baroque, it houses the famous Pappenheim altar, a huge medieval depiction of the Crucifixion. In the Willibald choir you can see the tomb of the missionary saint with its movingly realistic carving of St Willibald portrayed in old age.

The town's other main sight is the Willibaldsburg, the huge fortress palace built by the Prince-Bishops who ruled from 1355 until 1755. The most intriguing exhibit in the museum inside consists of the fossil remains of a 4m-long prehistoric crocodile.

90km northwest of Munich, 28km northwest of Ingolstadt. Tourist office: Domplatz 18. Tel: 08421 7977. Museum: April to September, Tuesday to Sunday 9am–noon, 1–5pm; October to March, 10am–noon, 1–6pm.

INGOLSTADT

Still guarded by the triple walls of its early-15th-century fortifications and by the Kreuztor of 1383, Ingolstadt lies picturesquely beside the River Danube. The city's cathedral of Our Lady, the Liebfrauenkirche, is a massive brick building finished in 1520. Entered by a flamboyant Gothic south porch, it boasts exuberantly carved choir stalls and pulpit, as well as late 15th- and early 16th-century stained glass. Later in date is the baroque Asam-Kirche Maria de Viktoria, whose ceiling, frescoed by Cosmas Damian Asam, is a masterpiece of perspective. Johann Michael Fischer created its magnificent high altar, which has statues representing medicine, theology, mathematics and philosophy.

Memories of the city's importance as a garrison town on the Danube are evoked by the Paradeplatz, laid out for military displays and overlooked by the moated Herzogschloss, founded by Duke Ludwig the Bearded in 1418. The castle now serves as the Bavarian Army Museum (open: daily except Monday 9.45am–1.30pm).

In Rathausplatz you will find the hospice church, the Spitalkirche, founded by Ludwig the Bavarian in 1319. In the same square are the city's twin town halls, one dating from 1592, the other created from four Gothic houses in 1882. Behind the town hall, in Moritzstrasse, stands the Gothic church of St Moritz, with a silver Madonna by Ignaz Günther and stucco work by Johann Baptist Zimmermann.
75km north of Munich. Tourist office: Hallstrasse 5. Tel: 0841 3051098.

NÖRDLINGEN

Nördlingen is the capital of the area known as the 'Ries', a circular crater some 25km in diameter created by a meteorite which crashed here some 15 million years ago. The city is protected by circular ramparts, built in the 14th century, five gates and 16 towers. The finest view of Nördlingen, and of the surrounding Ries, is from the 90m-high tower of the church of St George. The tower is nicknamed 'Daniel' and there are 365 steps to the copper dome at the summit, added in 1539. Opposite the church of St George is the half-timbered Tanzhaus, a building of the 1440s formerly used by the drapers for selling their goods during Nördlingen's Whitsun fairs, which drew traders from all over Germany. The statue placed over the entrance in 1513 represents Emperor Maximilian I, an orb in his right hand, his left hand resting on his sword.

Exquisite 16th- and 17th-century houses – some half-timbered, others baroque – ring the medieval heart of the city, situated around the Marktplatz. Here you will find the Rathaus, Nördlingen's town hall. This was built in the 13th and 14th centuries and was initially the venue for the town's Whitsun Fair. In 1618 Wolfgang Wallberger added its magnificent open staircase.

To find out more about the town you can visit the Stadtmuseum, housed in the 16th-century hospice of the Holy Ghost (open: December to February, Tuesday to Sunday 10am–noon and 1.30–4.30pm; closed Monday and January).
100km northwest of Munich. Tourist office: Marktplatz 2. Tel: 09081 84116.

Circular ramparts, with circular towers, ring the heart of medieval Nördlingen

Nürnberg

Nürnberg (Nuremberg in English) was one of the great medieval cities of Germany but it was heavily bombed during World War II (after which the name of Nuremberg became synonymous with the Nazi war-crimes trials). Nuremberg has now been rebuilt in such a way as to preserve the best of the former city within the modern one. Eighty towers rise from the city walls, whose outer ring dates from 1400, and irregular streets lead down to ancient bridges over the River Pegnitz. Today's city, the second largest in Bavaria, has a population of 500,000 and is a worthy successor to that which once nurtured the master singer Hans Sachs, the artist Albrecht Dürer, the brilliant metalworker Peter Vischer and the sculptors Veit Stoss and Adam Kraft.

Dürer-Haus

Albrecht Dürer (1471–1528), one of the finest Renaissance artists of Northern Europe, bought this house in 1509 and lived here for the rest of his life. Here he created many of his superb engravings (including charming and naturalistic depictions of rabbits). The museum in the house is devoted to Dürer's work. *Am Tiergärtenertor. Tel: 0911 162271. Open: March to October, Tuesday to Sunday 10am–5pm; November to February, Tuesday to Friday 1–5pm, Saturday and Sunday 10am–5pm. Admission charge.*

Hauptmarkt

Every weekday, farmers from the area around Nuremberg come to the city to sell their produce in the Hauptmarkt, the main market square. Another attraction is the cathedral clock with its 16th-century figures of the seven German Electors of Germany who pay homage to the Holy Roman Emperor. Near by stands Nuremberg's greatest fountain, the triple-tiered Schöner Brunnen, which was created by Heinrich Parler. Among its 40 sculpted figures are nine Old Testament heroes, the Four Evangelists, Charlemagne, King Arthur and the four Fathers of the Church.

Museums

Nuremberg has numerous museums to suit all interests. The Germanisches Nationalmuseum is packed with works of art, including masterpieces by Cranach and Dürer. The Spielzeugmuseum has the world's biggest and most varied

Characterful Nuremberg, birthplace of Dürer, has risen from the ashes of war

Playful Bacchic figures revel amongst the spray at Nuremberg's Schöner Brunnen Fountain

collection of historic toys, appropriate for a city that was regarded as the toy-manufacturing capital of Europe until World War II. Railway lovers should visit the Verkehrsmuseum (Transport Museum) to see Germany's first steam locomotive, the *Adler*.

Full details of all museums are available from the tourist office, Hauptmarkt 18. Tel: 0911 23 36132.

St Lorenz

One of the few Nuremberg churches to survive the bombing of World War II, the 13th-century building, with its twin spires, contains reproductions of two outstanding masterpieces: Adam Kraft's massive tabernacle (1493) and a carving of the *Annunciation* (1517) by Veit Stoss. The originals of these two treasures can be seen in the 13th-century Nassau House, alongside, where they have been placed for safe-keeping.

Lorenzenplatz. Open: standard hours (see page 18).

St Sebald

On Rathausplatz, Nürnberg's oldest church (13th-century) contains the bronze and silver shrine of St Sebald, an outstanding work of art created by Peter Vischer and his sons. Guides will point out where Peter Vischer has sculpted his own self-portrait on the tomb.

Open: standard hours (see page 18).

Schloss

Also known as the Kaiserburg, this imperial castle was built between 1167 and 1495 and was the home of the emperors till 1571. All that one imagines in a medieval castle is here, including a 13th-century keep and a 53m-deep well. The terrace gives a superb view of Nuremberg.

Guided tours: April to September, daily 9am–noon and 12.45–5pm; October to March 9.30am–noon and 12.45–4pm.

Location: Nürnberg is 170km north of Munich.

Regensburg

*T*his city on the Danube emerged from World War II remarkably unscathed and in consequence it has over 1,400 medieval buildings. You could spend hours exploring its churches and its alleys lined with Italianate tower houses and stately mansions. Parts of Regensburg breathe antiquity; one is the spot where huge stone blocks were discovered bearing an inscription stating that the Roman Emperor Marcus Aurelius founded the fortress of *Castra Regina* here in AD179. Now a university town with 130,000 inhabitants, Regensburg welcomes visitors to explore its patrician houses, churches and galleries, and to join its citizens in skimming the Danube in canoes and motorboats.

Altes Rathaus

Regensburg's former town hall, in Rathausplatz, was begun in 1360 and has a baroque east wing, plus a Venus fountain in its courtyard, both dating from 1661.
Neue-Waag-Gasse. Guided tours on the hour, Monday to Saturday 9am–4pm, Sunday 10am–noon.

Dom St Peter

South Germany's finest Gothic cathedral was begun in 1250, after a fire destroyed an earlier one. The lace-like south and

Regensburg, on the banks of the Danube

north towers, begun respectively in 1341 and 1383, point 105m skywards and were completed only in 1869. The exterior is rich in medieval carving, especially the west doorway, which features statues of St George and St Martin, and the humorous figures known locally as 'the Devil and his Grandma'. The interior is enriched by 13th- and 14th-century stained glass. The 15th-century rib-vaulted Gothic cloister is a delight and the All Saints' chapel has mid-11th-century architectural features.
Domplatz. Open: standard hours (see page 18).

Goliath Haus

This 13th-century house takes its name from an exterior fresco of David and Goliath, painted by Melchior Bocksberger in the 1570s.
Goliathstrasse.

Porta Praetoria

The remains of this Roman gateway date from the time when the city was first founded in the reign of Marcus Aurelius in AD179.
Unter den Schwibbögen.

St Emmeran

Once the chapel of a Benedictine

monastery, the crypt of this church dates from the mid-8th century and its nave was exuberantly stuccoed and decorated in the 18th century by the Asam brothers. The monastery itself was acquired in 1812 by the Princess von Thurn und Taxis (whose family became immensely rich by running Germany's postal system), and she converted it into a palace. The family continued building until 1889, but retained the magical Gothic cloister.
Emmeransplatz.

Schottenkirche
Not a Scots church, as the name suggests, but one founded by Irish Benedictines who were thought to be Scottish. Dedicated to St James, the church has a Romanesque north porch and a crucifix of 1180.
Schottenstrasse. Open: standard hours (see page 18).

Stadtmuseum
The history of Regensburg is revealed through a wonderfully detailed scale model of the city, along with archaeological finds and works of art by members of the Danube school of painters, including Albrecht Altdorfer.
Dauchaplatz 2. Open: Tuesday to Saturday 10am–4pm, Sunday 10am–1pm.

Steinerne Brücke
The view across Germany's oldest stone bridge (built between 1135 and 1146) is breathtaking; it takes in the city's gateways and towers, the venerable old houses with their dormer windows and the two fretted spires of the cathedral.

Location: Regensburg is 118km northeast of Munich. Tourist office: Altes Rathaus, Rathausplatz. Tel: 0941 507 4410.

Apostles and angels guard the door to St Peter's, Regensburg's Gothic cathedral

WALHALLA
Downstream from Regensburg at Donaustauf is this extraordinary national monument, modelled on the Parthenon in Athens and built in white marble in the woods beside the Danube. It was the brainchild of King Ludwig I and built to honour the great and good of Germany's long history, whose portrait busts are displayed within. You can reach the monument by car or, better still, by boat along the Danube (though you must climb 358 steps from the pier).
   Boat trips depart regularly throughout the day from Regensburg from June to September; the journey lasts 45 minutes each way. Details from the tourist office.

Time stands still in Rothenburg ob der Tauber, Bavaria's most romantic town

ROTHENBURG OB DER TAUBER

The most romantic town in Bavaria is perched above the winding River Tauber and surrounded by 2.5km of medieval walls, along which you can walk. Time seems to have stood still here since the 16th century.

The focal point of the town is Marktplatz. Here you will find the arcaded Rathaus (Town Hall), half of which is 13th-century Gothic, the other half Renaissance, having been built in 1578 by Leonhard Weidemann. It has a splendid tower dating from the 16th century with views from the top. Inside the Town Hall are dungeons, a gruesome torture chamber and a Gothic-style Imperial Hall where justice was dispensed (open: tower, daily 9am–12.30pm and 1–5pm; Town Hall, 8am–6pm).

The Ratstrinkstube of 1446 stands to the right of the Rathaus. In the baroque gable end there is a shuttered window which opens several times a day (at 11am, noon, 1pm, 2pm, 9pm and 10pm) to reveal mechanical figures who re-enact a pivotal moment during the Thirty Years' War; one figure represents the Catholic General Tilly who agreed not to sack the town if the Bürgermeister (Mayor) could drink three litres of wine in one draught. The Bürgermeister succeeded in downing the wine and for this feat the city was saved.

The tallest building in Rothenburg is the church of St Jakob, in Kirchplatz, a 14th-century basilica whose two crocketed spires rise high above the town's red-tiled roofs. It has many treasures, including 14th-century stained glass and a mid-15th-century high altar

on whose panels Friedrich Herlin painted scenes from the legend of St James the Great, incorporating into one panel a picture of Rothenburg in the 15th century. Above all the other treasures, this church shelters a *tour de force* by Tilman Riemenschneider, the Holy Blood Altar, which was carved in 1505 and depicts the Last Supper. Open 10am–noon (Sundays 10.30am) and 2–4pm; admission charge.
84km west of Nürnberg. Tourist office: Marktplatz. Tel: 09861 40492.

STRAUBING

Gabled houses, the 14th-century belfry (68m high) in the main square, Stadtplatz, and a Renaissance fountain all add charm to Straubing, so that one can readily forget that in 1445 the local duke had his wife, Agnes Bernauer, drowned in the river, erroneously suspecting her of witchcraft. In penitence for this he built a chapel for her in the atmospheric cemetery of St Peter's, the town's fine Romanesque church. Equally splendid is Jakobskirche, a magnificent Gothic church built of brick and designed by Hans Stethaimer. It has 15th-century stained glass and frescos, as well as baroque decoration by the Asam brothers and an 85m-high belfry. In the town museum you can see a rich hoard of Roman treasures, including gold masks, probably buried when the site, now occupied by the town, served as a frontier post on the Danube.
47km southeast of Regensburg. Tourist office: in the Rathaus on Stadtplatz. Tel: 09421 16307.

WEIDEN

Situated in the valley of the Waldnaab, Weiden is a sizeable place, with modern residential and industrial quarters surrounding an attractive old town. It was founded in the early 13th century on the trading route between Prague and Nuremberg and it greatly profited from this strategic position in the next two centuries. Evidence of this is the Altes Rathaus (Old Town Hall), a gabled building of 1539–45, with an octagonal tower topped with a Renaissance dome. Equally impressive is the Altes Schulhaus (Old Schoolhouse), a seven-storey building dating from 1566.

The two belfries of Josephskirche rise high above the houses of Weiden, and although it is a neo-Romanesque building of 1900, the interior is pleasingly decorated in the Bavarian art nouveau style called Jugendstil.
97km north of Regensburg. Tourist office: in the Altes Rathaus. Tel: 0961 81411.

Enjoying the outdoor life outside Weiden's Altes Rathaus

The Romantische Strasse

Germany's oldest, most beguiling tourist road stretches for 350km from Würzburg in the north-west, via Augsburg to Füssen in the south on the Austrian border. The road passes through so many entrancing medieval and Renaissance villages and towns that you could take a week or more to drive the route if you stop at all the destinations described below.

Leave Würzburg (see pages 124–5 and 128–9) by the B27 and drive southwest for 32km to Tauberbischofsheim.

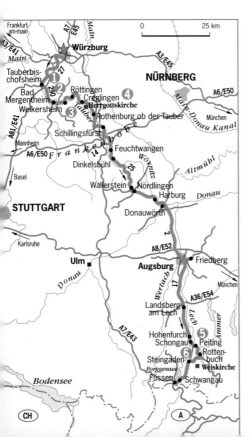

1 TAUBERBISCHOFSHEIM

Set in the Tauber valley, this is an unspoiled wine village of half-timbered houses, some sculpted with mermaids. Franconian wines can be sampled in the basement of the 14th-century castle, which also houses a local history museum (open: Easter to mid-October, daily except Monday 2.30–4.30pm). *Drive 18km southeast on the B290 to Bad Mergentheim.*

2 BAD MERGENTHEIM

The more modern spa town flourishes alongside the older town where you can see the Renaissance Deutschorden-schloss, the castle of the Grand Master of the Order of Teutonic Knights (open: March to October, daily except Monday 2.30–7.30pm, Sunday 10am–noon). Several Grand Masters lie buried in the crypt of the 18th-century castle church (by Balthasar Neumann and François Cuvilliés).
Green signs, with lettering in yellow, now direct you along the route. After driving east for 11km on the B19 you reach Weikersheim.

3 WEIKERSHEIM

The town is dominated by the moated Renaissance palace of the Hohenlohe family, who ruled the region, with its magnificent baroque garden.
Continue east through half-timbered Röttingen, shortly turning south to reach Creglingen.

4 CREGLINGEN

Just outside the town is the Herrgottskirche, a church of 1380 housing Tilman Riemenschneider's masterpiece, the 7m-high Altar of Our Lady, carved out of limewood in 1505.
Drive 18km southeast on the B25 to Rothenburg ob der Tauber (see page 106). The route now continues southeast through the baroque town of Schillingsfürst, medieval Feuchtwangen, Dinkelsbühl, Nördlingen, and Donauwörth. The B2 takes you to Augsburg (see page 82). The route then continues on the B17 through Landsberg am Lech (see page 88), Hohenfurch and the walled health resort of Schongau with its fjord-like lake. The Romantische Strasse then arrives at Peiting.

5 PEITING

This market town, situated between the Rivers Ammer and Lech, is a popular winter sports centre. In summer it makes a good walking base – local shops sell the hiking map (*Wanderkarte*) that details a hike along the so-called King Ludwig's Route to Rottenbuch. Alternatively, drive on to this town.

6 ROTTENBUCH

The interior of the church of Maria Geburt, all that remains of an Augustinian convent founded in 1074, is a rococo confection by local artists including the accomplished Matthäus Günther.

Bad Mergentheim's Renaissance castle

The route continues west to Steingaden, with its Romanesque monastery and the nearby pilgrimage Wieskirche. This is one of the most magnificent rococo churches in Bavaria, its perfectly composed interior décor amongst the finest achievements of the Zimmermann brothers.
Finally the Romantische Strasse curves its way southwest to Schwangau (see page 92) and Füssen (see page 84).

Northern Bavaria

ASCHAFFENBURG

Aschaffenburg is a town of majestic buildings and green parks situated on a bluff alongside the River Main. Its Altstadt (Upper Town), located between the huge sandstone castle and the Stiftskirche, is blessed with twisting streets, welcoming inns and half-timbered houses. This town is the perfect starting point for excursions into the Spessart forest.

Schloss Johannisburg

Once the residence of the Electors and Bishops of Mainz, this huge building of red sandstone was designed by Georg Ridinger of Strasbourg and built between 1605 and 1614. Today it serves as the city art gallery and the fine state rooms are hung with works by German and Flemish artists, most notably Lukas Cranach. Some of the rooms have preserved their original furniture, much of it dating from the late 18th century.

Open: April to September, daily 9–11.30am, 1–4pm; October to March, daily 10–11.30am, 1–3.30pm. Closed: Monday.

Schönbusch Park

Laid out in the 18th century, this is one of Germany's oldest formal gardens. The park is enlivened by a little castle set beside a lake, by a classical temple, pavilions, a maze and a restaurant.

NORTHERN BAVARIA

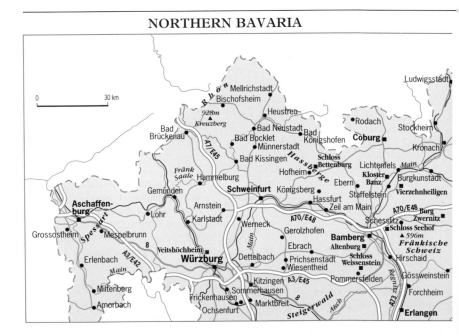

Schloss Johannisburg, Aschaffenburg, built as a palace for the Bishops of Mainz

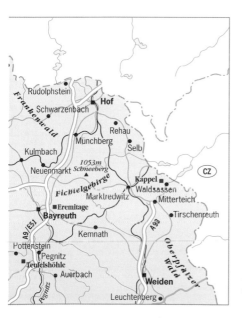

Sportscar Museum Rosso Bianco
This claims to display the largest collection of sports cars in the world – 200 or so classic vehicles built for speed and good looks. The museum also displays posters and other memorabilia of the golden age of the automobile.
Obernauer Strasse 125. Open: April to October, Tuesday to Sunday 10am–6pm; November to March, Sunday and bank holidays 10am–6pm. Closed: Monday.

Stiftskirche St Peter und St Alexander
This is the oldest church in Aschaffenburg, built in the 12th century, with a late Romanesque cloister and a 15th-century tower. It houses a 12th-century crucifix and a rare painting – *Lamentation* by Matthias Grünewald. *Dalbergstrasse. Open: Monday to Saturday 9am–dusk, Sunday morning service and noon–dusk.*

Location: Aschaffenburg is 70km northwest of Würzburg. Tourist office: Schlossplatz 1. Tel: 06021 395800.

Bamberg

Set like Rome on seven hills, the university city of Bamberg rose to prominence nearly 1,000 years ago. Heinrich II, who became Holy Roman Emperor in 1014, regarded this as his favourite city and lies buried in its cathedral. The River Regnitz divides the city into its ecclesiastical and its secular parts, though the former town hall, entrancingly straddling the river, symbolically unites them. The virtually traffic-free island on the Regnitz hosts a flea market on Untere Brücke, presided over by a statue of Heinrich II's wife, St Kunigunde. A new concert hall has been built for the city's symphony orchestra. Bamberg has 10 breweries and four beer gardens (to which you can take your own food), while a half-hour trip down the River Main takes you to the Franconian vineyards.

Alte Hofhaltung

The former prince-bishops' residence, next to the cathedral, with its Renaissance façade and Gothic interior courtyard, is now the city's history museum.
Domplatz. Open: May to October, Tuesday to Sunday 9am–5pm; open for exhibitions during winter. Closed: Monday.

Altenburg Schloss

Situated on the highest of the city's seven hills, with its moat, battlemented walls, keep and neo-Gothic chapel, the former bishop's castle is fronted by an 18th-century Crucifixion group by Georg Adam Reuss.
Open: May to October, Tuesday to Sunday 9am–5pm. Closed: Monday.

Carmelite monastery

The late-Romanesque cloister dates from the 13th century, while the rest of the buildings are baroque, transformed by Leonhard Dientzenhofer in 1692.
Karmelitenplatz. Open: daily 8.30–11.30am and 2.30–5.30pm.

Kaiserdom

The four Gothic towers of the city's great 13th-century cathedral dominate the splendid Domplatz (Cathedral Square). On the Princes' Portal expressive carvings depict the *Last Judgement*.

Among the cathedral's superb works of art is the Bamberger Reiter (Bamberg Knight), an exquisite equestrian statue sculpted around 1230. In the west chancel is the tomb of Pope Clement II (the only papal tomb north of the Alps). The sarcophagus of Emperor Heinrich (Henry) II and his wife, Kunigunde, was created in 1513 (some 450 years after their deaths) by Tilman Riemen-schneider. Another superb group of medieval carvings in the cathedral shows the Jewish Synagogue (a blindfolded woman), the Christian Church, and the Virgin Mary and her cousin Elizabeth. The south transept contains the celebrated Marienalter (1523) carved by Veit Stoss, with the tiny infant Jesus watched over by his mother. The cathedral museum is in the chapter house built by Balthasar Neumann in 1730.
Domplatz. Open: standard hours (see page 18); museum open daily 9am–6pm; to 5pm in winter.

Kleine Venedig

Stretching downstream alongside the

River Regnitz from Bamberg's Rathaus (Town Hall) is a row of fisherfolk's houses. These are part of the water-lapped and picturesque quarter known as Bamberg's Little Venice, which is often floodlit at night.

Neue Residenz

This huge baroque building was created for Prince-Bishop Lothar Franz von Schönborn between 1697 and 1703 by the architect Johann Dientzenhofer. Its most imposing room is the Emperor's Hall, but all the rooms are splendidly decorated in baroque style. Behind the building is a Rose Garden with a view of the former Benedictine abbey of St Michael.

Domplatz. Open: daily April to September 9am–noon, 1.30–5pm; October to March, 9am–noon, 1.30–4pm.

St Michael

Towering on a height above the city, this church was once the chapel of a Benedictine monastery and now has a superb baroque façade and flight of steps by Leonhard Dientzenhofer. Inside, Romanesque pillars support Gothic vaults (painted with 600 pictures of medicinal herbs). The pulpit of 1751 is by Georg Adam Reuss. The other monastic buildings (by Dientzenhofer and his brothers and Balthasar Neumann) now shelter an old people's home, two restaurants and a brewery museum.
Open: Thursday to Sunday 1–4pm.

Location: Bamberg is 61km north of Nuremberg. Tourist office: Geyerswörth Strasse 3. Tel: 0951 871161.

Bamberg's Altes Rathaus

Bayreuth

*A*lthough Bayreuth today is universally associated with Wagner, its musical traditions date back to the early 15th century and the rule of Margrave Friedrich I. In the 17th century his successors, the Margraves of Brandenburg-Kulmbach, decided to make Bayreuth their principal home, enticing here Italian and Prussian, as well as Bavarian, musicians. In the mid-18th century one of the Margraves married the cultured Princess Wilhelmina of Prussia, elder sister of Frederich the Great, who inspired the court with new artistic standards. In 1764 her husband commissioned an architect from Bologna, Giuseppe Galli-Bibiena, to build an opera house, and it was this lovely building that entranced Richard Wagner in 1871 when he was seeking a concert hall large enough to mount his Ring cycle. Franz Liszt, father of Wagner's wife Cosima, was another composer attracted to Bayreuth; today he lies buried in the town's cemetery.

Altes Schloss

The older of Bayreuth's two castles was begun in the 14th century but was largely rebuilt in the 1750s. Its 18th-century chapel was designed by the French architect François Joseph de Saint-Pierre.

The town that Wagner made his home

Maximilianstrasse. Open: April to September, daily 9–11.30am, 1–4.30pm; October and March, 10–11.30am, 1–2.30pm. Closed November to February.

Festspielhaus

Wagner had this Festival Hall built in 1872–76 on a hill north of the town. The pink and white building resembles an amphitheatre and seats 1,800 people. It hosts the annual Bayreuth Wagner Festival in late July and August.
Grüner Hüger. Open: summer 10–11.30am, 1.30–3pm. Tel: 78780.

Haus Wahnfried

Richard Wagner built this villa for himself in 1873. It now serves as a museum dedicated to his life, his music and his friends, including Mathilde Wesendonck who inspired *Tristan and Isolde*. Wagner and his wife Cosima are buried in the villa grounds.
Richard-Wagner-Strasse. Open: daily 9am–5pm.

Markgräfliches Opernhaus

This opera house, built by Giuseppe

Neues Schloss and its accompanying dramatic fountain

Galli-Bibiena in the 1740s, is infinitely more seductive than the one built for Richard Wagner. Its galleried interior is a superb mélange of baroque reds, golds and greens.
Opernstrasse. Open: daily except Monday 9–11.30am (from 10am in winter), 1.30–4pm.

Neues Schloss
Built in the mid-1750s, the Schloss is full of finely decorated rooms and galleries, including a Japanese Room and a Hall of Mirrors. It faces on to a fantastical fountain designed by Elias Räntz in 1700. The pictures in the Schloss demonstrate Princess Wilhelmina's love of Asian art. In addition you can see works from the Bavarian national picture collection. Behind the castle is the Hofgarten, a fine park laid out in 1609.

Ludwigstrasse. Guided tours April to September 10–11.30am, 1.30–4.30pm; October to March 10–11am, 1.30–3pm.

Location: Bayreuth is 67km northeast of Nuremberg. Tourist office: Luitpoldplatz 9. Tel: 0921 88588.

EREMITAGE
Situated 4km east of Bayreuth is the 18th-century Eremitage (Hermitage), where members of the court would go to dress up as shepherds and shepherdesses. In its park is a rococo Temple of the Sun, a Hermit's Chapel, a Dragon's Den, several fountains and cascades and the grave of Wilhelmina's pet dog, Folichon, built in the form of a medieval ruin.

WAGNER IN BAVARIA

In 1861 the future King Ludwig II of Bavaria (see page 94) heard Richard Wagner's opera *Lohengrin* and was entranced. Almost immediately after becoming king in 1864 he promised Wagner (then in hiding from his creditors) that he would 'banish from you the petty cares of everyday life,

allowing you to spread the mighty wings of your genius'. The degree to which Ludwig II idolised Wagner is clear at Schloss Hohenschwangau (see page 92), where Ludwig entertained his protégé and which is crammed with Wagner memorabilia (including the composer's piano and his bust set next to a gilt-framed portrait of the king), while at Neuschwanstein (see pages 92–3) the rooms are decorated with scenes from the composer's greatest operas.

Ludwig paid off Wagner's debts, for which the composer was enormously grateful: 'Long after we are dead,' wrote the composer, 'our work will continue to delight and dazzle the centuries.' Wagner's next opera, *Tristan und Isolde*, was staged at Munich in 1865 and was a triumph.

Their friendship proved disastrous for the king, however, for Wagner's revolutionary connections alarmed the monarch's advisers. They were even more concerned at the amount of money the king was spending on his friend and in 1865 the two men were forced to part.

Ludwig had planned a Wagnerian opera house in Munich but was forced to abandon the project. Wagner set about raising his own funds to build a theatre in Bayreuth (spurning as too small the exquisite baroque Markgräfliches Opernhaus, even though it had initially attracted him to the town). Aided by massive loans he eventually succeeded in building the Festspielhaus (see page 114), which opened in 1876 with the first complete perfomance of his three-part work, *Der Ring der Nibelungen*.

Management of the Festspielhaus has remained within the hands of the Wagner family ever since. At Wagner's death in 1883, his widow Cosima took over. She was followed by their son, Siegfred, who also composed operas. Siegfred's wife, Winifred Williams, directed the Bayreuth Festival until 1944. Wagner's grandsons, Wieland and Wolfgang, took over in 1951, and Wolfgang became the theatre's sole director after Wieland died in 1966.

Scenes from *Die Meistersinger* decorate the walls of Schloss Neuschwanstein

A pleasant courtyard within the Veste Coburg fortress

COBURG

In the 19th century Coburg's dukes and duchesses had the knack of marrying well. Among their number was Prince Leopold of Saxe-Coburg, who became the first king of Belgium in 1831. One of his sisters married the Duke of Kent, and their daughter, Victoria, ascended the British throne in 1837. Queen Victoria then married Prince Albert of Saxe-Coburg. Other scions of the family succeeded to the thrones of Portugal, Belgium and Bulgaria. The town of Coburg is dominated by the splendid Veste (Fortress), which was home to this illustrious family until they moved into the Ehrenburg in the lower town.

Ehrenburg

The ducal residence from 1547 to 1918, this castle is part Renaissance and part 19th-century neo-Gothic. The splendid Giants' Hall is so called because of the 28 plaster figures that hold up the ceiling.

Schlossplatz. Guided tours: daily 10am, 11am, 1.30pm, 2.30pm, 3.30pm and 4.30pm (last tour 3.30pm November to March). Closed Monday.

Puppenmuseum

This appealing museum displays doll's houses, dolls and toys dating from 1810 to 1950.

Rückerstrasse 3. Open: April to October, daily 9am–5pm; November to March, Tuesday to Sunday 10am–5pm.

Veste Coburg

One of Germany's largest and best-preserved medieval fortresses, Veste Coburg sits on a spur high above the town. Because of its tower-studded outline, it is often called the 'Crown of Franconia'. Dating back to the 11th century, most of the present fortress was rebuilt in the 16th and 17th centuries. In 1530 the Protestant reformer Martin Luther took refuge here, and you can see the room where he stayed.

Veste Coburg houses a massive collection of engravings, some 350,000 in total, representing every European school. You can also see displays of hunting weapons and weapons of war, carriages, furniture, glassware, porcelain and paintings from the Middle Ages to the 20th century.

Guided tours: April to October, Tuesday to Sunday 9.30am–1pm, 2–5pm; November to March 2–5pm. Closed: Monday.

Location: Coburg is 100km north of Nuremberg. Tourist office: Herrngasse 4. Tel: 09561 74180.

HASSFURT

Still partly surrounded by its medieval fortifications, Hassfurt retains its remarkable grid of streets, laid out in chequerboard fashion in the 13th century. Most of the town's buildings date to the 16th century. One of these is the three-storeyed Rathaus (Town Hall) of 1521 with its stuccoed hall and portraits of the prince-bishops who ruled the town.

The 14th-century Ritterkapelle served the nobility of Hassfurt and is copiously decorated with their coats of arms – 248 of them on a frieze and 28 others sculpted on the keystones of the arches.

Rising in the town's main square, Marktplatz, the parish church of St Kilian was founded in 1390. Sadly the baroque interior was destroyed in the 19th century to make way for a neo-Gothic refashioning, but some lovely treasures remain inside the building; they include two masterpieces by Tilman Riemenschneider, a statue of the Virgin

Hassfurt's Gothic church of St Kilian

and another of St John the Baptist.

The hilly country surrounding Hassfurt, which lies between the Hass mountains and the Stieger woods, is criss-crossed with hiking routes and sprinkled with ruined castles.
30km northwest of Bamberg. Tourist office: in the Rathaus. Tel: 09521 688227.

HOFHEIM

Hofheim is a town of charming half-timbered houses situated on the western side of the Hass mountains. Among these houses is the Apotheke, a pharmacy built in 1581. The parish church is a late-Gothic building which houses a sculpture of St Mary and St John (1460), as well as some fine baroque statues.
14km north of Hassfurt, 45km northwest of Bamberg. Tourist office: Marktplatz. Tel: 09523 92290.

SCHLOSS BETTENBURG

Some 3km north of Hofheim, the castle has stood here since 1343 and was mostly rebuilt from 1537. In the 19th century Christian Truchsess von Welzhausen transformed the Schloss into a music centre.

KRONACH

The most celebrated son of Kronach was the artist Lucas Cranach the Elder, who was born here in 1472 and who went on to become court painter to the Protestant Elector Friedrich the Wise at Wittenberg.

The most historic part of Kronach, with its medieval heart, is the picturesque upper town. Here you will find the Altes Rathaus (Old Town Hall), a Renaissance building with a 17th-century entrance and numerous coats of arms carved in stone. There are guided tours available on request.

Above the town rises the mighty Schloss Rosenberg, a 12th-century medieval fortress with a triple ring of walls and only one entrance. It was redesigned by Balthasar Neumann in the 1730s as a refuge for the Bishops of Bamberg, to which city Kronach belonged for 700 years. Part of it is now a youth hostel, while its south wing houses the Frankische Galerie, a branch of the Bavarian National Gallery, devoted to Franconian art from the Middle Ages to the Renaissance. On show are sculptural masterpieces by Tilman Riemenschneider, Veit Stoss and Adam Krafft (open: April to December, daily except Monday 10am–5pm).

45km northwest of Bayreuth. Tourist office: Marktplatz 5. Tel: 09261 97236.

KULMBACH

This quaint old town has a famous brewery producing Kulmbacher Eisbock – said to be the strongest beer in the world. It is overlooked by the Veste Plassenburg, the finest Renaissance fortress in Franconia. The mid-12th-century castle was rebuilt mainly by Caspar Vischer in the 1560s. Today it houses the Zinnfigurenmuseum, a

national collection of some 300,000 tin figurines (open: April to September, Tuesday to Sunday 10am–5pm; October to March 10am–3pm; closed: Monday).

23km northwest of Bayreuth. Tourist office: in the Rathaus. Tel: 09221 82216.

OCHSENFURT

Literally translated, Ochsenfurt means 'ox ford', though today you do not have to wade across the River Main – it is spanned by the Mainbrücke, a bridge built of wood in the 13th century and later replaced in stone. The town retains its well-preserved 14th-century fortifications and many picturesque half-timbered houses, especially along Hauptstrasse and Brückenstrasse. Its emblem is the clock tower in the town hall whose mannequins have performed for the citizens since 1560.

The clock figures merely enhance the most entrancing late-Gothic town hall in Franconia. Construction of the Rathaus began at the start of the 16th century, and the eight-sided clock tower (topped with a spire) was added in 1560. Dormer windows and an open-air staircase with elaborate balustrades all add to the ambience, while the Councillors' Hall has a painted Renaissance ceiling. The Stadtmuseum, also housed within the town hall, has a stirring display of ancient weapons and other local history memorabilia (open: daily 10am–noon, 2–4pm).

Another important building is the impressive 13th-century church of St Andreas which still retains its tower of 1288, though the chapels were not finished until the late 15th century and the chapel dedicated to St Johann Nepomuk dates from the 18th century. The spacious Renaissance high altar of

Ochsenfurt's pretty main street leads to the splendid Rathaus

1612 is the masterpiece of a relatively unknown sculptor, Georg Brenck, who was born in Windsheim. The church's octagonal bronze font was created in the 1720s. The finest sculpture in St Andreas is Tilman Riemenschneider's carving of St Nicholas.

20km south of Würzburg. Tel: 09331 5855.

POMMERSFELDEN

Pommersfelden is famous as the location of Schloss Weissenstein, one of Bavaria's most sumptuous palaces. The Schloss was built between 1711 and 1718 by Johann Dientzenhofer for Prince-Bishop Lothar-Franz von Schönborn, who held many positions and titles, including those of arch-chancellor of the Holy Roman Empire, Bishop of Bamberg and Archbishop-Elector of Mainz. Later on, his palace was further enhanced by the skills of the Mainz architect Maximilian von Welsch and the Viennese architect Johann Lukas von Hildebrandt, court architect to the Habsburgs.

The central building, with its imposing entrance hall, is flanked by two wings and looks on to a formal garden and courtyard (the Ehrenhof) as well as the crescent-shaped mews which Maximilian von Welsch added in 1714. The supreme glory of this palace is its staircase. Prince-Bishop Lothar-Franz himself dabbled in architecture and, with the help of von Hildebrandt, designed this staircase himself. The double flight of stairs rises to the first floor, which is surmounted by two galleries overlooking a huge well. In 1718, J R Byss decorated its ceiling with a *trompe l'oeil* depiction of the four corners of the world, surveyed by the ancient Greek gods of Olympus.

Other treats are the Grotto Hall, lit by chandeliers and decorated with stucco sea shells and leaves, a pink dining room, a Hall of Mirrors and the marble hall, which rises to the height of five storeys. This last displays portraits of the Schönborn family as well as idealised depictions of Italian artists. The Banqueting Hall is still laid out for ghostly 18th-century personages to sit and eat. Dispersed throughout the Schloss are paintings by such masters as Rembrandt, Peter Paul Rubens, Titian, Albrecht Dürer and Peter Brueghel. Schloss Weissenstein also has a restaurant, and hosts concerts from July to mid-August.

26km south of Bamberg. Tours: April to October, Tuesday to Sunday 9am–noon, 2–4pm. Closed: Monday.

KLOSTER BANZ

On a plateau rising on the opposite side of the River Main to Vierzehnheiligen is the monastery of Banz. Founded in 1069, the monastery was ruined in the Thirty Years' War and rebuilt by Johann Leonhard Dientzenhofer, assisted by his brothers and by Balthasar Neumann. The monastery chapel is superbly frescoed and contains sumptuous furnishings. There are also splendid views from the church terrace over the Main valley to Vierzehnheiligen.

VIERZEHNHEILIGEN

In the mid-15th century, 14 saints (*Vierzehnheiligen* in German), along with the Infant Jesus, repeatedly revealed themselves to a devout shepherd named Hermann Leicht who lived beside the River Main just south of Lichtenfels. He inspired the abbot of nearby Banz to build a little pilgrimage chapel high on the left bank of the river, on the spot where they had appeared.

Two centuries later this chapel was attracting so many pilgrims that Balthasar Neumann was commissioned to build a new church big enough to accommodate them all. Along with his pupils and the Italian fresco master Appiani, Neumann created what can only be called the most outrageously

The central pavilion of Schloss Weissenstein in Pommersfelden

successful baroque church in Germany, though the rather plain and conventional exterior gives no clues as to the fanciful decoration within. Your sensibilities are likely to whirl once you step inside this sensuous building. Everything is a delightful froth of well-lit stucco decoration painted pink, white and gold. The focal point is J M Küchel's altar, depicting the 14 saints, which goes over the top in dazzling wildness, though Appiani's ceiling frescos well match this exuberance. Nothing here is placid, everything is overwrought, yet the whole is coherently brilliant.

Between Staffelstein and Lichtenfels, 30km northeast of Bamberg. Open: standard hours (see page 18).

Würzburg

*T*he history of this ancient university town stretches back to 1000BC, when Celts first built a hill fort on the heights now occupied by the Marienberg fortress. Würzburg derives its name from the Castellum Virteburg founded by the Franks in the mid-7th century. Irish missionaries, led by St Kilian,' were martyred here in 689, having failed to convert the inhabitants to Christianity, but the town was the seat of a bishop from 742, and in 1168 Frederick Barbarossa elevated them to the status of prince-bishops. The university was founded in 1582, and after the Thirty Years' War the prince-bishop of the day' fortified the city and began building the superb Residenz.

This, and other fine buildings, earned Würzburg the title 'Jewel of the Main'. Disaster struck the city, however, in March 1945 when an air raid left the centre almost entirely destroyed. Würzburg today is a university and business city that cherishes its ancient heart and preserves numerous celebrated inns serving the local Franconian wine. The city straddles both banks of the River Main, the two halves linked by the ornate Alte Mainbrücke (the Old Main Bridge). Most of the sights of the old town on the west bank are described in the walk on page 128. In addition, there are the following sights dotted around the edges of the city.

Würzburg's Residenz, built for the town's powerful prince-bishops

Festung Marienberg

Festung Marienberg began life as a hill fort around 1000BC, and from then on the hill always had some kind of fortification on its summit. The present fortress has Renaissance and baroque elements, and the armoury of 1712 now houses the superb Mainfränkisches Museum, whose works of art include masterpieces by Tilman Riemenschneider (see page 126). In the Princes' Wing (the Fürstenbau) an exhibition recounts the history of Würzburg over the last 1,200 years.

Museum open: April to October, Tuesday to Sunday 10am–5pm, closing at 4pm in winter. Closed: Monday. Fürstenbau open: April to September, Tuesday to Sunday 9am–12.30pm, 1–5pm, closing at 4pm in winter. Closed: Monday. Admission charge.

Käppele

This pilgrimage church on the west bank of the Main escaped bombing because of its relatively isolated position. It was built by Balthasar Neumann in 1748 and has a sumptuous interior with stucco work by Joseph Anton Feuchtmayr and frescos by Matthäus Günther.

Residenz

Designed by Balthasar Neumann, this

WÜRZBURG

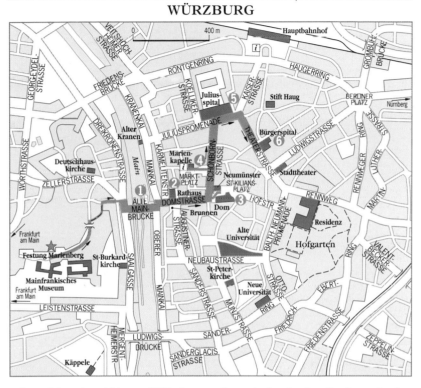

palace of the prince-bishops of Würzburg constitutes one of southern Germany's greatest baroque buildings. It was built between 1720 and 1744 with the help of Maximilian von Welsch and the Viennese architect Lukas von Hildebrandt. The triumphal staircase rises beneath a cantilevered dome which is painted with a huge ceiling fresco by the Venetian artist Giovanni Battista Tiepolo. The Emperor's Hall also has frescos by Tiepolo, and he was responsible for the altar paintings of the lavish court chapel. The gardens are filled with statues and have magnificent rococo wrought-iron gates (see page 134).

Open: April to October, Tuesday to Sunday 9am–5pm, closing at 4pm in winter. Closed: Monday. Admission charge.

Stift Haug

Built between 1670 and 1691, and boasting twin spires and a dome, this was the first baroque church to be built in Franconia, its architect the Italian Petrini. Over the main altar is a Crucifixion painted in 1683 by the Venetian painter Tintoretto.

Location: Würzburg is 103km northwest of Nuremberg. Tourist office: Am Congress Centrum. Tel: 0931 37335.

BAVARIAN CARVING

Bavaria's greatest sculptor, Tilman Riemenschneider (1460–1531), came to Würzburg in 1483 and eventually rose to become Bürgermeister (Mayor) of the town. Many of his limewood, marble and sandstone masterpieces are displayed in the Mainfränkisches Museum in Festung Marienberg (see page 124). They include his sandstone figures of Adam and Eve, which are among the most tenderly humane works of the late medieval period.

Another of his superb sculptures, representing the Virgin and St John weeping over the dead body of Christ, is to be found in Würzburg's Martin-von-Wagner Museum. For the parish church of Hessenthal in the Spessart he carved another quite different, equally exquisite *Lamentation*. Other masterpieces include the tomb of St Heinrich and St Kunigunde in Bamberg cathedral (see page 112) and his entrancing carving of the Madonna in the pilgrimage church at Volkach.

Perhaps his greatest work is the Holy Blood Altar (so-called because it houses a crystal containing what is alleged to be a drop of Christ's own blood) carved between 1501 and 1505 for the church of St Jakob, Rothenburg ob der Tauber (see page 106). In this work, which depicts the *Last Supper*, Jesus and his disciples are individually characterised, while the wings of the altarpiece dramatically represent Jesus's triumphant entry into Jerusalem on Palm Sunday and his anguish on the Mount of Olives.

Left: the carving tradition continues in
modern Oberammergau

Above: tomb carving in Bamberg's cathedral
Below (left) limewood carving by Tilman
Riemenschneider and (below) saintly figures in
Würzburg's Mainfränkisches Museum

Riemenschneider stands in a long tradition of Bavarian carving, as can be seen from the statues in Bamberg cathedral (see page 112). His contemporary, Veit Stoss, sculpted a sublime *Annunciation* which can be seen in Nuremberg cathedral (see page 102), while another contemporary, Erasmus Grasser, created the delightful set of folk dancers now displayed in Munich's Stadtmuseum (see page 50). Two decades later the brilliant Hans Leinberger was working in Landshut (see page 69), where he carved the *Landshut Madonna* and a superb tomb for the church of St Martin.

Bavaria's baroque master carvers matched the accomplishments of their medieval predecessors. Even minor artists, such as Ignaz Weibel who carved the prior's stall (1691) for the Klosterkirche at Buxheim, produced masterpieces. And the Bavarian woodcarving tradition lives on, particularly at Oberammergau.

A Walk in Würzburg

This walk takes you through the lively heart of old Würzburg. See page 125 for a map of the route. *Allow 1 hour.*

Start at Festung Marienberg (see page 124). After enjoying a panoramic view of the old city, walk from the Marienberg down to the Alte Mainbrücke.

1 ALTE MAINBRÜCKE

Built between 1473 and 1543, the Alte Mainbrücke spans the River Main and is adorned by numerous statues of saints added in the 18th century. They include the Virgin Mary (patron saint of Franconia), the infant Jesus and St Joseph, St John Nepomuk (patron saint of bridges, since he was martyred by drowning), St Burkard the first Bishop of Würzburg, and King Pepin and his son Charlemagne, the first Holy Roman Emperor.

To the north of the bridge, beside the river, you will spot an ancient crane (Alte Kranen), once used for unloading trading

ships, which dates to around 1770, close to which is the House of Franconian Wines. As you walk up Domstrasse from the bridge you will see a baroque fountain created in 1765 by L von der Auvera and Peter Wagner, sculpted with figures representing the four Cardinal Virtues and topped by a statue of the Virgin.

2 RATHAUS

The town hall rises beside its fountain. It has a 55m-high Romanesque tower, and the Wenceslas Hall (named after the king of Bohemia) dates to the 13th century. The Roter Bau (Red Building), a late Renaissance building of 1659 with a baroque façade, adjoins the Rathaus.

Today the city council meets in the south wing of the town hall, while the Ratskeller serves food and drink in the open central courtyard.

Follow Domstrasse up to St-Kilians-Platz, site of one of Germany's largest Romanesque cathedrals.

3 THE DOM AND THE NEUMÜNSTER

The cathedral of St Kilian, begun in 1040, is dedicated to the Irish missionary who arrived here in AD686. It was later enriched by a 15th-century Gothic cloister and by the chapel of the Prince-Bishops of Würzburg. Inside are sculptural masterpieces by Tilmann Riemenschneider (especially a carving of Rudolf von Scherenberg). Just north of the cathedral stands the Neumünster, built over the grave of St Kilian, with its curving baroque façade and its sweeping staircase. Founded in the 12th century, the church was totally rebuilt in the early 18th century by Johann Dientzenhofer.

Left: the panoramic view of the old city from the Festung Marienberg

Walk north along Schönbornstrasse and turn left into the city's main square, Marktplatz.

4 MARIENKAPELLE

This Gothic building that dominates Marktplatz is decorated with statues of Adam and Eve, copies of Riemenschneider's original, now in the Mainfränkisches Museum (see page 124). Near the entrance is the tomb of Balthasar Neumann, the city's greatest architect, and there are several fine medieval knights' tombstones within. *Return to Schönbornstrasse, turn left and walk to Juliusspital at the end.*

5 JULIUSSPITAL

This imposing almshouse was founded in 1576 by Prince-Bishop Julius Echter and reconstructed after a fire of 1699 by the Italian baroque architect Antonio Petrini. It incorporates a rococo pharmacy, with sculptures by Johann Peter Wagner, and a baroque fountain of 1706, symbolising Franconia's four rivers and designed by Jakob van der Auvera. In the atmospheric cellars you can buy wine by the glass, by the carafe or by the bottle. *Turn right along Juliuspromenade and first right into Theaterstrasse to find the Bürgerspital, halfway down on the left.*

6 BÜRGERSPITAL

An even older charitable institution than the Juliusspital, the Bürgerspital was founded by rich citizens in 1316 to care for the town's aged and needy. It still does and, like the Juliusspital, derives its income chiefly from selling the wines of its extensive vineyards. The Bürgerspital is also blessed with a Gothic church, housing precious carvings, and an arcaded early-18th-century courtyard.

Flora and Fauna

*T*he best way to learn about Bavaria's rich wildlife is to explore one of the region's national parks (see pages 136–8).

Animals

Some of the more unusual animals to survive in the Nationalpark Bayerischer Wald (Bavarian National Forest) are pine martens, wildcats and red squirrels, spied on by eagle owls or the shy lynx. The Hass mountains are a breeding ground for birds of prey, while wild boars roam the woods. Among the Alpine animals treasured here are the chamois, the mountain hare, salamanders, various species of rare woodpecker and the black grouse.

Plants

Violet and yellow gentians (distilled at Berchtesgaden to make *Enzian* liqueur) are just two of the striking species that dot the lower slopes of the Alps. As you climb in late winter, you may see hellebores (Christmas roses) peeping out of the ground. You may admire – but are not allowed to pick – the many different species of rare Alpine plants. The locals still believe that certain plants have magical properties; kitchens in the Berchtesgaden region, for instance, are decorated with willow stems because they are reputed to fend off witches.

Alpine gentians flower during July and August

GETTING AWAY FROM IT ALL

> 'Those whom love you,
> Lord, let them live in
> this land.'
> **LUDWIG GANGHOFER**
> 1855–1920

Getting Away From it All

PARKS AND GARDENS

Bavaria abounds in superb parks, often set around palaces, many of them dating from the period following the Thirty Years' War (1618–48) when the region's gardeners were influenced by the French baroque style (and above all by the gardens of Louis XIV's palace of Versailles). Towards the end of the 18th century gardens became less formal and far more picturesque; this was the period when the so-called 'English' style was developed, particularly by Friedrich Ludwig von Sckell.

Spring colours in the borders of Ansbach's delightful Hofgarten

ANSBACH

The Hofgarten was laid out as a baroque garden in the first half of the 18th century and landscaped in the 1780s. The 18th-century orangery is fronted by colourful flower-beds (see page 98). *Open: daily from sunrise to sunset. Free.*

ASCHAFFENBURG

Beside the River Main, 3km west of the town, is Schönbusch, a park laid out in 1778 around a Schloss belonging to the Archbishop of Mainz. It was designed by Joseph Emanuel d'Herigoyen and later landscaped by Friedrich Ludwig von Sckell. Scattered throughout the park are picturesque follies, such as shepherds' huts and Dutch-style cottages, which pleasingly contrast with the other classical buildings (see page 110). *Open: daily. Free.*

BAYREUTH

Bayreuth boasts two superb gardens. The first surrounds Schloss Eremitage, so called because the castle was built to resemble a monastery, or hermitage, in 1715. A second castle in the same garden was completed in 1753. Grottoes, water-jets and fake ruins (such as a 'Roman' theatre) dot the park, which was laid out from 1736 and later landscaped in the English fashion (see page 114). *4km northeast of Bayreuth. Open: daily. Free.*

The second garden, called Sanspareil, was laid out in the mid-18th century as a 'wild' park, with beech trees, rock formations and rustic buildings. *On the A505 between Bayreuth and*

Bamberg. *Open: April to September,*
Tuesday to Sunday 9am–noon, 1.30–5pm.
Closed: Monday.

LINDERHOF

Laid out by Karl Effner in the 1880s to
surround one of King Ludwig II's castles
(see page 94), these gardens reveal the
king's passion for all things French. The
ornamental flower-beds take the shape of
Bourbon lilies while the western and
eastern parterres have busts of Louis XIV
and Louis XVI respectively. Cascades
flow down the steeply terraced slopes.
The 'Venus Grotto' has an underground
lake and tableaux simulating the first act
of Wagner's opera *Tannhäuser*. Ludwig
also bought a Moorish kiosk from a
Berlin railway magnate and erected it in
the garden.
20km south of Oberammergau. Open: daily
9am–12.15pm, 12.45–5.30pm in summer,
to 4pm in winter. Gardens free.

MÜNCHEN

The city has numerous parks and
gardens, including the Englischer Garten
(see page 36), and the Alter Botanischer
Garten near the station. The best are
those of Schloss Nymphenburg (page 58)
and Schloss Schleissheim (see page 60).

Schloss Nymphenburg

As initially laid out by its two French
gardeners, the baroque style of the park
surrounding Schloss Nymphenburg, with
its lovely pools, deliberately mimicked
the garden of Versailles without slavishly
copying it. Though Friedrich Ludwig
von Sckell was to landscape the park at
the start of the 19th century, he did not
entirely obliterate the original baroque
design.
Open: April to September, daily 7am–8pm,
closing at 5pm in winter. Gardens free.

Set beside Schloss Nymphenburg is a
botanical garden, laid out in 1914 for the
Bavarian Science Academy. Here you
can study at close quarters specimens
of the plants that grow in the region,
including Alpine plants, rhododendrons,
heathers and ferns.
Open: April to September, daily 9am–9pm,
5pm in winter. Free.

Schloss Schleissheim

The attractive baroque garden of
Schloss Schleissheim is the work of
Dominique Girard, a French designer
who had worked at Versailles. It has a
splendid cascade which falls to a sunken
parterre.
Open: daily. Gardens free.

A non-floral exhibit in Munich's Alter
Botanischer Garten

WEIHENSTEPHAN
This major horticultural garden is located just south of Freising and displays some 800 varieties of rose and 250 types of paeony as well as numerous hardy perennials, shrubs and ornamental trees. *Open: daily. Free.*

WÜRZBURG
Hofgarten
Balthasar Neumann conceived the notion of integrating the long façade of the Residenz with the old fortifications of Würzburg by means of a lavish garden embodying subtly created terraces (see page 124). In 1774 Johann Prokop Mayer, court gardener to Prince-Bishop Adam Friedrich von Seinsheim, began work on the eastern section of this sumptuous garden. He created the terraces, joined together either by flights of steps or by ramps. Sculptures and balustrades add to the glamour, as do arbours of larch and laburnum.

Mayer next turned his attention to the south garden. Terminating in an orangery, this garden was later landscaped in the English style, informally incorporating lawns and trees. Some of the latter are magnificent, including clipped pyramids of 200-year-old yew trees, as well as cypresses, magnolias, limes and plane trees and an avenue of oriental ginkgos. *Open: daily. Free.*

Schloss Veitshöchheim
The baroque palace in this village, 7km north of the city, was built by the prince-bishops of Würzburg as their summer residence. Here, in the 1760s, Prince-Bishop Adam Friedrich von Seinsheim commissioned Johann Prokop Mayer to design what eventually became Germany's finest surviving rococo garden. He was able to utilise the Grosser See, a large formal lake already created by 1703, as well as some baroque elements of the earlier garden which Balthasar Neumann had designed. A grid of hedges and walks, arbours and Chinese pavilions, and statuary by Peter Wagner and Ferdinand Tietz complete an exquisite ensemble of 18th-century garden design.
Open: April to September, Tuesday to Sunday 7.30am–8pm; in winter 8am–4pm. Closed: Monday. Garden free.

LAKES AND RIVERS
In Oberbayern (Upper Bavaria) the waters of over 20 lakes ripple amid superb mountain and tree-clad scenery. Watersports are allowed on most of the lakes, though such activities are banned on some in order to preserve the plant and animal life along their shores. Sports flourish particularly on the Ammersee, the Chiemsee (see page 66), the Starnberger See, the Schliersee and the Tegernsee. Some Bavarian lakes are exceedingly cold because of their depth, while others, such as the Auwaldsee, the Riegsee, the Schliersee, the Staffelsee and the Wörthsee, are warm enough to make sport and swimming a pleasure in summer.

Starnberger See
The region around the Starnberg Lake is dubbed the Fünf-Seen-Land ('Five Lakes Land') and its lakeside towns are readily reached from Munich using the S-Bahn 5 or 6 trains. A typically attractive resort catering for these lakes is the fishing village of Münsing, situated on a ridge between the Isar and the Starnberger See. Here a 13km stretch of the lake's shore is reserved for holidaymakers, with activities ranging from surfing to steamship excursions.

Lindau's pretty lakeside harbour on the Bodensee (Lake Constance)

Bodensee

At the extreme southwest of Bavaria, Lindau borders the Bodensee (Lake Constance), where you can swim, windsurf, water-ski and fish. Though close to the Alps, this is a curiously mild region, with orchards and outdoor cafés by the lakeside. You can also take a boat trip to the island of Mainau, which has been transformed into a floral park full of orchids, tulips, dahlias, lilies, roses, rhododendrons and many other species.

East Allgäu

Further east are the four major lakes of the East Allgäu (all of them visible from Schloss Neuschwanstein – see page 92): the Forggensee, the Schwansee, the Hopfsee and the Bannwaldsee. The region is in fact washed by 30 lakes in all, whose shore length totals some 115km.

Bad Tölz

Five per cent of the Bad Tölz region consists of lakes, amongst the most popular being the Tegernsee, the Walchensee, the Bibisee (near Königsdorf) and the Kirchsee (close to Sachsenkam).

Entrancing towns and villages guard the shores of these lakes. A visit to Kochel am See, beside the Walchensee, offers the chance of fishing, sailing, rowing, surfing and swimming.

Danube tours

A cruise along the Danube offers welcome relief from hectic tourism. Passau is an excellent starting point, and you can choose from a variety of tours, including an 8-day return trip to Budapest, or a 4-day return trip to Vienna.

In summer, Regensburg is a centre for shorter cruises along the Danube, for example to Walhalla or Mariaort. Kelheim is a third centre, from which you can sail as far as Regensburg through some of the river's most spectacular reaches.

Cruises from Passau are arranged by the Agentie Passau, Im Ort 14a (tel: 0851 33035) or Wurm & Köck, Höllgasse 26 (tel: 0851 929292). For information about cruises starting at Regensburg apply to the local tourist office, the Fremdenverkehrsverein, Altes Rathaus, 93047 Regensburg (tel: 0941 5074411). Kelheim has several

cruise companies, among them Schiffahrtsgesellschaft Kelheim Steibl, Fischergasse 21 (tel: 09441 3201) and Schiffahrtsgesellschaft Stadler, Postfach 93301, Kelheim (tel: 09441 8290).

NATIONAL PARKS

Bavaria rejoices in several national parks which are managed in such a way as to leave the ecosystems as undisturbed as possible while granting access to serious visitors. Among Bavaria's finest national parks are the following.

ALTMÜHL WILDLIFE PARK

Rare plants, birds and butterflies inhabit the juniper- and grass-covered heathlands of the Altmühl valley. Fossil-hunters are encouraged, and you can borrow geological hammers in the quarries of Eichstätt-Blumenberg and Mörnsheim-Apfeltal. Once completely covered by the sea, the valley is rich in fossils and skeletons dating back to 150 million years ago (the fossil skeleton of the oldest known bird, *Archaeopteryx*, was found here and is preserved in the Bürgermeister-Müller-Museum at Solnhofen).

The Altmühl Wildlife Park information office is housed in a former monastery at Eichstätt (tel: 08421 6733).

AUGSBURG'S WESTLICHE WÄLDER NATURAL PARK

This is Swabia's sole nature park, covering 115,500 hectares and bordered by the Rivers Danube, Lech and Mindel. The terrain is hilly and comprises tree-shaded slopes rising up from gentle meadows watered by softly flowing streams. Around 40 per cent of the park is under forest which shelters animals and plants, some of them rare.

Since 1984 the Westliche Wälder

Befreiungshalle (Freedom Monument) commemorating Napoleon's defeat overlooks the Altmühl Valley

Natural Park information office has been accommodated in the baroque Oberschönfeld Cistercian monastery at Gessertshausen (tel: 083238 2912), where you can obtain information about the climate, woods and meadowland, soil and colonisation, and also the flora and fauna of the park (open: daily, except Monday and Friday, 10am–5pm; closed February and November).

Limestone mountains, beech woods and Alpine meadows at Berchtesgaden

BAVARIAN FOREST

The Bayerischer Wald is a vast national park with two open-air museums. Parts of it adjoin the Bohemian Forest (in the Czech Republic) to form the largest conifer-forested area in Europe. It climbs well over 1,000m above sea level (its finest peak the 1,456m-high Grosser Arber), affording visitors the opportunity for hang-gliding as well as the chance to view animals (no longer roaming free but kept in spacious enclosures at the centre of the park).

The baroque monasteries of Speinshart and Waldsassen add allure to the region, as do intimate villages and stern fortresses. Hotels, guest houses and private rooms welcome visitors, many of whom come in winter to ski along 300km of runs. To enable naturalists to study the exceptional flora and fauna of this region, there are 200km of marked walks, as well as geological zones set aside for those interested in studying the rock formations.

For further information contact the Bavarian Forest Nationalpark-Haus, 94556 Neuschönau (tel: 08558 1300).

BERCHTESGADEN NATIONAL PARK

Bordering on the Austrian province of Salzburg, this park, established in 1978, is some 210sq km in extent. Ancient limestone mountains surround its exquisite lake. Deciduous forests (mostly of beech) cover almost half the park and are a spectacular sight in autumn when their leaves turn to gold. The beech forest grades into conifers, such as spruce and pine, at higher elevations. These forests rise as high as 800m, while at 1,800m and above rare Alpine vegetation scrapes a living among the rock debris and crevices. Alpine meadows alternate with areas of alder and dwarf pine. Lakes and rivers wash the region. Open to visitors throughout the year, the park has 190km of marked paths and climbing routes as well as several mountain huts with catering facilities.

The Berchtesgaden National Park information offices are at Franziskaner-platz 7, Berchtesgaden (tel: 08652 64343), and in the former railway station at Schönau am Königssee (tel: 08652 62222).

DIRECTORY

'Every traveller who has an ear
and a heart will notice that as
he passes through Bavaria, everyone
sings and the bells ring out.'
CHRISTIAN FRIEDRICH/DANIEL SCHUBART
in 1785

Shopping

MUNICH

Huge department stores mix with elegant boutiques and useful everyday supermarkets in the shopping complex of Karlsplatz (also known as Stachus) in Munich. Munich is also an international fashion centre, and if you want expensive clothing you should head for the elegant shops along Maximilianstrasse and Theatinerstrasse.

Both men and women will be attracted to **Loden-Frey** in Maffeistrasse, the premier Munich outlet for traditional Bavarian costumes, such as Loden-coats made out of long-lasting, thick, weatherproof green cloth, matched by feathered hats. Diagonally opposite the shop is the rococo-fronted **Wallach-Haus**, its name deriving from Moritz Wallach who began producing the city's famous hand-printed materials in 1900; its store is crammed with these lovely fabrics as well as attractive souvenir tablecloths.

Parts of Munich resemble one huge antique market, particularly the area round Ottostrasse and Briennerstrasse, while cheaper bargains are to be found in Türkenstrasse in Schwabing (to the west of the Englischer Garten). Schwabing remains a student area, and its characterful off-beat shops, between Münchener Freiheit and the Siegestor, claim that 'the unusual is always in fashion'.

BEYOND THE CAPITAL

One of Augsburg's most charming recent innovations has been the transformation

Chic shopping in a typical central Munich department store

of the narrow streets and medieval houses of the Untere Stadt into a shopping area full of antique shops and boutiques, while two other pedestrianised zones house modern shops. Looking for traditional dress, try the **Dirndlstube-Trachtenmoden** shop of Gretl Glöckl at Annastrasse 25.

Aschaffenburg is another Bavarian town that has made its main shopping centre into a pedestrianised precinct, and at Regensburg the ancient ambience of the Altstadt, the upper town, is enhanced by a multitude of small shops, the larger department stores being reserved for the more modern part of the city.

A noted centre for antiques, Bamberg boasts many dealers specialising in baroque art (try those in Karolinenstrasse). The city has also revived its tradition of fine weaving. There is a noted flea market on the island in the middle of the River Regnitz between the two parts of the city.

Above: toys for the children and (below) clothes for dressing up older boys and girls in the Schwabing area of Munich

Nuremberg has numerous fashionable boutiques and department stores, and it attracts bargain-hunters to its annual September flea market, which sells antiquities, bric-à-brac and art. Jewellery, glass and porcelain are also good buys here.

At Würzburg you should buy Franconian wine. The best sources are the **Bürgerspital** on the corner of Theaterstrasse and Semmelstrasse; the **House of Franconian Wines** at Kranenkai 1; the **Hofkeller** in the Rosebach Palais on Residenzplatz; and the **Weineck Julius Echter** (the outlet of the Juliusspital) at Köellikerstrasse 1–2.

Crafts

In some parts of Bavaria traditional crafts have never died out. In others they are being vigorously revived – for example at Nördlingen where you can watch a cooper making barrels according to ancient methods.

Augsburg's tourist office supplies a guide to the city's workshops where you can watch crafts being produced – the tour includes visits to silversmiths, a violin maker, the embroidery workshops of the Dominican nuns, a tannery, and a rope maker. For details and times apply at the Verkehrsverein,

The honourable and ancient Bavarian craft of woodcarving

Bahnhofstrasse 7 (tel: 0821 502071).

Oberammergau specialises in carvings of Christmas crib figures, crucifixes, and statues of the Virgin and various saints. Here, too, you can see workshops specialising in the crafts of painting on glass and modelling in wax.

The craft of glass-blowing has, for centuries, been a speciality of several centres in the Bavarian Forest. You can see demonstrations in Neustadt bei Coburg (northeast of Coburg, beyond Rödental) at the Inge-Glas Weihnachtsland factory (Dieselstrasse 7; tel: 09568 540).

Mittenwald, in Oberbayern, dubs itself the Village of a Thousand Violins, a tradition deriving from 1683 when a local farmer's son, Mathias Klotz, returned home after many years working in Cremona with the celebrated violin-maker Nicolo Amati and handed on his skills to others in the town. Today the violas and cellos of Mittenwald are exported worldwide. Few, perhaps, can afford a violin as a souvenir, but the same region, especially around Berchtesgaden, also specialises in affordable hand-painted boxes, known as *Spanschachteln*, as well as wooden dolls and figurines.

Kulmbach (see page 120) not only has a museum devoted to tin figures, it also hosts a tin-figure exchange market each August. By contrast, Bayreuth's favourite metal is pewter, its symbol the Bayreuther Eichala, a hand-crafted tankard with an acorn on its lid.

At Nuremberg the half-timbered boutiques and workshops lining the narrow streets of the Handwerkerhof (Artisans' Courtyard) offer high-quality

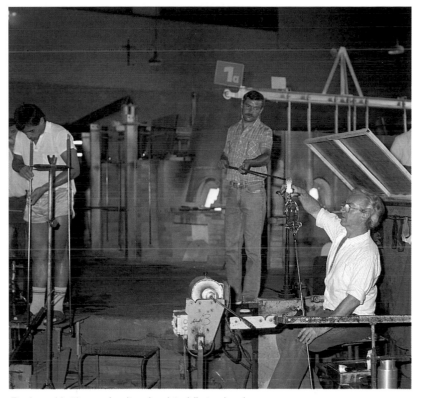

Turning red-hot lumps of molten glass into delicate wine glasses

wares of traditional craftsmanship: ceramics for the house and garden; glassware; the creations of goldsmiths, silversmiths and tinsmiths; purses, belts and other leather goods; engravings; toys and dolls; and elaborate candles. Amongst these Nuremberg's chief fame lies in its traditional wooden toys.

Since so much of Germany's porcelain tableware is produced in the area around Fichtelgebirge, in Franconia, the region has set up a Porcelain Route (the Porzellanstrasse) through the major manufacturing centres of the region. Information can be obtained from the tourist office at Bayreuther Strasse 4, 8591 Fichtelberg (tel: 09272 6255).

Finally, delightful kitsch is displayed in the world-famous Maria Innocentia Hummel figures. Made by W Goebel Porzellanfabrik (Coburger Strasse 7, 96472 Rödental, northeast of Coburg; tel: 09563 92303), these immensely popular porcelain recreations of innocent children of yesteryear were designed by a Franciscan nun who was born in Bavaria in 1909.

TRADITIONAL BAVARIA

DANCE

Folk dances in Bavaria are far subtler than the traditional image of people slapping their clogs and each others' cheeks (sometimes promulgated in a tongue-in-cheek fashion by the Bavarians themselves). These dances are characteristic only of Bavaria's southernmost regions. Other regions have preserved their own rich dance traditions. In Lower Bavaria at fairs and festivals you come across more than 100 different dances. The Upper Palatinate specialises in *Zweifachen*, a dance with changes in rhythm, whereas in Upper Franconia open-air folk dancing (especially at the fairs) culminates in Bavaria's fastest dance, which is rightly dubbed 'The Gallop'.

MUSIC

Dialect songs are still popular in Upper Bavaria, where regional Christmas carols are especially prized. Traditional musical instruments – the zither and the alpenhorn, for instance – add charm to Bavarian folk evenings.

COSTUME

Bavarians so relish their national costumes that throughout the Free State, hundreds of national costume clubs have

been formed. Each region of Bavaria has its own distinctive costume, the result of their origins. In Franconia, for

Many aspects of Bavarian folklore are part of a living tradition enjoyed (and sometimes satirised) by every generation

example, the national dress dates back, in the main, to the 18th century, so that when the citizens bring out their finest garb for festivals and fairs the aspect is baroque. In the Alpine regions, by contrast, traditional costumes for the most part have developed out of hunting clothes. Upper Bavarians can be recognised by their leather shorts, their feathered hats and their woollen jackets.

TRADITIONS

Centuries-old traditions remain unchanged in parts of Bavaria. One example is the feast of St Michael the Archangel, known as Michaeli, celebrated in the Bavarian Alps on 29 September. This is the date on which cowherds traditionally bring their animals down to the safety of the valleys before the advent of the winter snow. Dressing in traditional costumes, they also deck the heads of their beasts with crowns created from flowers and sprays of spruce and larch.

Entitainment

*B*avaria offers a wide variety of top-class entertainment, ranging from classical ballet to pop and jazz. This is true not only of Munich, but of all the major cities, and even quite tiny villages. The list which follows covers only the major centres and inevitably omits some entrancing spectacles, but local tourist offices amply supply the visitor with details of what is happening.

MUNICH
The city mounts an opera festival from July to the beginning of August. Summer concerts frequently take place in the city's fine palaces, particularly Schloss Nymphenburg, Schloss Blutenburg and the castle at Dachau.

What's on?
Around the 22nd of each month the Munich tourist office publishes an inexpensive official monthly programme (*Monatsprogramm*) which can be obtained in the tourist office, at newspaper stands and in many book shops. This lists theatre, music and exhibition schedules.

Classical music and theatre
Classical and modern plays are performed in the Residenztheater and in the Kammerspiele im Schauspielhaus (Maximilianstrasse 26). The Bavarian State Opera House (the Nationaltheater on Max-Joseph-Platz) hosts ballet and occasional concerts as well as opera. Smaller operas are also staged in the Cuvilliés-Theater. The Gasteig-Kulturzentrum (Gasteig Cultural Centre) boasts a fine new concert hall. Light opera, operetta, musicals and ballet are performed in the Staatstheater am Gärtnerplatz.

Free concerts
Students of the Richard Strauss Conservatory play free of charge in the Kleine Konzertsaal of the Gasteig Cultural Centre on weekdays from

Inviting night lights

Munich's splendid Cuvilliés-Theater is used for chamber operas

1.45–2pm. Also free are many of the concerts given by the Music Academy at Arcisstrasse 12.

Specialist theatres

Munich's youth theatre (Theater der Jugend) is located at Franz-Joseph-Strasse 47. For avant-garde theatre, visit the Marstalltheater and Werkraumtheater.

Rock and pop

The favourite venues for rock and pop concerts are the Olympic Hall, the Kongresssaal of the Deutsches Museum, the Circus Krone and the Alabama Hall.

Tickets

For opera and other performances at the Nationaltheater, the advance sales office is at Maximilianstrasse 11 (open: Monday to Friday 10am–1pm, 2–6pm; Saturday 10am–1pm). In the evenings you can buy tickets at the theatre box office, which opens an hour before each performance (two hours on Sundays), and which offers reductions for students, so long as the performance is not sold out. You can also buy cheaper tickets provided that you are willing to stand and watch.

The box office at the Staatstheater am Gärtnerplatz is open Monday to Friday 10am–12.30pm, 3.30–6pm, Saturday 10am–1pm, with cheap tickets for standing room. The Staatstheater box office opens an hour before performances. The Olympic Hall box office in the Ice Stadium, Olympic Park, opens Monday to Saturday 10am–6pm (tel: 089 5481 8181). Buy tickets for the Cuvilliés-Theater at the Residenz, Residenzstrasse 1 (tel: 089 220868), and for the Gasteig Cultural Centre at Rosenheimer Strasse 5, where the box office opens Monday to Friday 10.30am–2pm, 3–6pm; Saturday 10.30am–2pm (tel: 089 418 1614).

AUGSBURG

Proud of its Mozart connections, Augsburg offers concerts in the house where the composer's father, Leopold, was born, along with readings from Wolfgang's letters to his cousin. In addition, the Augsburg Wind Quartet and the Augsburg String Quartet regularly give performances in the city. For information enquire at Bahnhofstrasse 7 (tel: 0821 502070).

The city mounts candlelit concerts of chamber music in the rococo ballroom of the Schaezlerpalais in August and September (Maximilianstrasse 46; for information tel: 0821 324 2730). Chamber music is also performed in the mid-18th-century Kleiner Goldener Saal (Jesuitengasse 9; for advance booking arrangements see the local press).

From pop to gospel and the big band sound

The Stadttheater (City Theatre), on Kennedyplatz 1 (tel: 0821 36604), stages opera, ballet and drama, while the Kongresshalle (Congress Hall) is the venue for symphony concerts (Gögginger Strasse 10; tel: 0821 324 2348). The Kömodie hosts plays and ballet and has a studio for plays and chamber music (Vorderer Lech 8; tel: 0821 36604). The Freilichtbühn stages opera and operetta (Am Roten Tor 5; tel: 0821 36604). All theatre booking offices open for ticket sales one hour before performances begin. To book (up to five days) in advance for any of these theatres call at the vestibule of the City Theatre on weekdays between 10am–1pm and 5–6pm. Check with the Augsburg tourist office for up-to-date information or other assistance. Augsburg tourist office also publishes a useful annual preview (*Veranstaltungskalender*) of each year's happenings.

BAMBERG

In June and July the municipal theatre leaves its usual home, the E T A Hoffmann Theater on Schillerplatz (tel: 0941 871433), to mount the open-air Calderon Festival in the courtyard of the Alte Hofhaltung (the former Residenz beside the cathedral). The theatre also has a studio at Markusplatz 7 (for advance bookings tel: 0941 871433).

Bamberg also has its own symphony orchestra and a youth orchestra, both of which perform in the city's Kulturraum. Organ concerts are regularly given in the cathedral. Information from the tourist office (Geyerswörthstrasse 3; tel: 0951 871161).

BAYREUTH

Trumpet fanfares announce the opening of the festival which Richard

Wagner founded at Bayreuth in 1876. Undoubtedly this remains the most prestigious annual musical event in Bavaria. The festival runs from late July through August, but you will stand little chance of finding a seat unless you apply the previous October to the Festspielhaus (Siegfried-Wagner-Allee, 8580 Bayreuth). Along with the tickets the local tourist board will send a list of hotels; rooms should be booked at once, because they become very scarce during the festival. Bayreuth does not slumber for the rest of the year – it has a full programme of musical events including, for example, a spring festival known as the Fränkische Festwoche.

COBURG

Coburg's Landestheater am Schlossplatz (formerly the Court Theatre) seats 500 and is host to varied productions, including jazz, ballet and opera (box office tel: 09561 92742). Opposite stands the Studio Theatre (the Reithalle), which mounts modern drama.

On the Tuesday after Whitsun Coburg also mounts its annual Market Festival, dominated by student fraternities. There is also a funfair, the Vogelschiessen, in the week before the beginning of the annual school summer holidays (usually mid-July), when competitors vie for the title 'King of Marksmen', a tradition deriving from the foundation of the Coburg Marksmen's Club in 1354.

The tourist office (Herrngasse 4; tel: 09561 74180) publishes the monthly *Coburg Aktuell*, listing the happenings in the town.

The huge Philharmonic Hall in Munich's Gasteig-Kulturzentrum

LINDAU

The Stadttheater in Barfüsserplatz is notable for being a former convent church. Here the Bodensee Symphony Orchestra performs, alternating with chamber music ensembles and a selection of international plays – the emphasis being on 20th-century dramatists such as George Bernard Shaw, Bertolt Brecht, Jean Anouilh and Arthur Miller.

For information about performances and local events ring the tourist office (tel: 08382 260030).

NUREMBERG

The Nuremberg Civic Theatre at Richard-Wagner-Platz 2 has three auditoria, including an opera house, and presents the whole range of musical drama, from classical to modern works (for information about performances tel: 0911 270 7536; for advance booking tel: 0911 22990). Experimental theatre is mounted in the new Tafelhalle (Äussere Sulzbacher Strasse 60; tel: 0911 598 8730 for advance bookings).

The Mastersingers Hall (Münchener Strasse 21; tel: 0911 492011) mounts pop and jazz as well as classical concerts. Other jazz venues are the Jazz Studio (Paniersplatz 27–9; tel: 0911 224384) and the Schmelztiegel (Bergstrasse 21; tel: 0911 203982).

Concerts in churches, in the Kaiserburg and in other historic sites around the city, are characteristic of the annual festival 'Summer in Nuremberg', which takes place from May to September (information from the tourist centre; tel: 0911 23360). Every even-numbered year the city hosts a major jazz festival, while classical, jazz and folk concerts take place throughout summer in the ruins of the church of St

Katharina. From May to October concerts are also arranged in the historic Knights' Hall of the Kaiserburg. Finally, Nuremberg is renowned for its international organ week, which lasts from the last week in June to the first week in July.

PASSAU

Since 1952 Passau has been staging a 'European Week' every summer – a blend of opera, operetta, music, ballet, pantomime, concerts, drama, public readings by distinguished writers and exhibitions. For information and tickets apply to the Kartenzentrale der Europäischen Wochen Passau, Nibelungenhalle, 8390 Passau (tel: 0851 33038).

The city's theatre in Gottfried-Schäffer-Strasse was once the prince-bishops' opera house (advance bookings, tel: 0851 929 1913). Passau's Theater im Scharfrichter Haus at Milchgasse 2 sponsors cabaret from October to December (tel: 0851 35900).

REGENSBURG

Regensburg's municipal theatre, where you can enjoy opera, operatta, plays and concerts, is at Bismarckplatz 7 (box office tel: 0941 59156). In addition the city has an open-air theatre in the courtyard of the Thon-Dittmer-Palais (tel: 0941 59156)) and mounts drama, cabaret, musicals and light entertainment in the Turm-Theater of the Goliath House (Watmarkt 5; tel: 0941 562223). Regensburg's folk theatre (Stadtamhof 5; tel: 0941 85958) is only for those who can understand plays in the local dialect. For cabaret try the Statt-Theater (Winklergasse 16; tel: 0941 53302; advance bookings at the tourist office, tel: 0941 507 4411).

Dramatic moments in Regensburg's municipal theatre

Jazz buffs come to Regensburg for the annual Bavarian jazz weekend, mounted at the end of July and attracting jazz bands from all over Bavaria.

WÜRZBURG

Every year, at the end of May, Würzburg's Residenz hosts a festival of baroque music; tickets for concerts include dinner accompanied by Franconian wines – book in advance by writing to the Fränkischer Weinbauverband, 8700 Würzburg. The city also presents an internationally renowned Mozart festival every year during the second and third weeks of June. Tickets are prized and hard to come by, but disappointed music lovers can take consolation from the free Kleine Nachtmusik concerts performed in the Residenz gardens during the festival period. In addition Würzburg sponsors a Bach week at the end of November in the church of St Johannis – for tickets apply to the Würzburger Kartenvorverkauf on the second floor of the clothing store Breuninger Am Kürschnerhof (tel: 0931 55554).

The Stadttheater (municipal theatre) – Theaterstrasse 21; tel: 0931 3908124) presents drama, ballet and opera, while lighter entertainment is on hand at the Theater Chambinsky (Valentin-Becker-Strasse 4; tel: 0931 51262).

Festivals

*B*avaria is a region of numerous festivals, many of them commemorating some decisive event in the history of the town or city. Beginning with Munich, the following are amongst the most diverting.

MUNICH

Fasching, the Shrovetide carnival, begins very early in the year in Munich – immediately after Christmas, in fact. On the Friday following 7 January the Fasching Princess is enthroned in the Deutsches Theater. On the Sunday before Shrove Tuesday clowns perform in the Marienplatz, and on Shrove Tuesday itself the stallholders of the Viktualienmarkt dance in costume, some of them dressed like the chickens they normally sell.

The Starkbierzeit, or 'Strong Beer' festival, lasts two weeks and traditionally takes place during the third and fourth weeks before Easter; during this time the various breweries produce beers of extra special strength. Another Munich beer festival, the Maibock, begins in the Hofbräuhaus on the last Thursday in April, while the celebrated Oktoberfest begins at the end of September (see page 42).

The Auerdult takes place three times a year in Mariahilfplatz, with markets selling shoes, clothing, ceramics and glassware, junk, books and antiques. Originally these were religious festivals; today they comprise the Maidult (lasting nine days from the Saturday before 1 May), the Jakobidult (lasting nine days from the Saturday preceding St James's Day, 25 July) and the Kirchweihdult (lasting nine days from the third Saturday in October).

AUGSBURG

Augsburg rivals Munich in its plethora of festive events, beginning with the Bärenbergl, a folklore and beer festival held in March, soon to be followed by the Easter beer festival. In May and June citizens dress in historic costumes for the Bürgerfest, which evokes the Renaissance splendours of the city. In July, Augsburg hosts a theatre festival, which combines mime, circus, comedy, dance, acrobatics and slapstick, while the end of August is the excuse for another beer festival.

BAD TÖLZ

St Leonhard is the patron saint of horses and on his feast day, 6 November, the town presents its annual Tölzer Leonhardifahrt, a procession of decorated carts pulled by majestic horses, accompanied by citizens in traditional costumes and brass bands

Anything goes during Munich's carnival

Decorative float (with obligatory beer) at the St Leonhard festival in Bad Tölz

blaring away. After the procession the citizens gather in the Marktstrasse to watch a display of whip-cracking using old coachmen's whips.

BAMBERG
In the second half of July, Bamberg's beer festival takes place on Maximiliansplatz. The city's 10 private breweries vie with each other to produce their finest local speciality, the *Rauchbier* or smoked beer, so called because the barley from which it is brewed is first cured over smouldering beech wood. The Bamberg Sandkerwa, a festival lasting five days at the end of August, involves members of fishermen's guilds from all over Bavaria

precariously jousting with long poles from boats on the River Regnitz.

BERCHTESGADEN
On the evening of 5 December, the night before the feast of St Nicholas, Berchtesgaden's menfolk dress as evil spirits for the Butt'nmandln festival, tying cow bells to their waists and pretending to frighten the children in their homes. These evil spirits are then defeated by St Nicholas, who comes to each house to check which children are in his gold book (giving these nuts, chocolates and oranges) and which are in his black book (in which case they are tumbled in the snow).

COBURG

On the Tuesday after Whitsun, the Marktfest is devoted to the antics of the Coburg student fraternities. The annual July Schlossplatzfest, set in the square in front of Schloss Ehrenburg, is a gastronomic treat organised by the leading city restaurants, with bands, actors, jugglers and dancers regaling you as you eat.

Nearby Sesslach (southwest of Coburg) hosts an Altstadtfest on the third weekend of August, when the streets of the upper town are filled with booths and the Marktplatz is enlisted as a beer garden.

At Rodach, northwest of Coburg, the third Saturday in December is welcomed by a Franconian Christmas, when the citizens parade through the town with lighted torches and hand out presents to the children in the Marktplatz.
(See page 149 also.)

DINKELSBÜHL

Dinkelsbühl was besieged eight times during the Thirty Years' War and was finally taken by the Protestant King Gustavus Adolphus. The pleadings of its children who, in 1632, marched out to the captors bearing only flowers, persuaded the victors to spare the town. The event is remembered in the annual mid-July Kinderzeche, which includes performances by a 50-strong boys' band dressed in splendid red and white rococo uniforms, echoing the colours of the town's flag.

KULMBACH

The town's beer festival, with brass bands in traditional costume and huge barrels set up in the Marktplatz, takes place in the first week of August.

LANDSHUT

In 1475 Hedwig, the 18-year-old daughter of the King of Poland, came to Landshut to marry the son of the local duke, Georg the Rich. For seven days every guesthouse and tradesman in Landshut served visitors free – at their duke's expense. The marriage was a triumph of pageantry. Since 1903 the people of Landshut have re-enacted this event, the Landshuter Hochzeit 1475, every third year, from the end of June to mid-July. Flags wave, flutes whistle, drums beat and dancers and jesters parade the streets in a pageant that involves over 2,000 participants dressed in early-15th-century costumes. Renaissance music plays in Burg Trausnitz and in the Residenz. The festival ends with knights in armour jousting.

NUREMBERG

Mid-September sees the city's Altstadtfest, which combines cultural and folklore events with irrepressible jazz and rock (for Nuremberg's other festivals, see page 150).

REGENSBURG

Once every two years, at the end of June, Regensburg celebrates its Bürgerfest with folk music, copious amounts of beer, jugglers, arts and crafts displays and theatre. In June several churches also participate in the annual Bach week. At the end of July the city also hosts a jazz festival with amateur bands from the whole of Bavaria.

ROTHENBURG OB DER TAUBER

The annual highlight of the year at Rothenburg ob der Tauber occurs on Whit Sunday with the celebration of the

One of the acts waiting to perform at Nuremberg's Altstadtfest

Meistertrunk. This pays homage to the town's Bürgermeister (Mayor) who persuaded General Tilly not to raze the town, during the Thirty Years' War, if he managed to drink the contents of a huge flagon of wine in a single draught.

STRAUBING

The Gäubodenfest at Straubing, held during the middle two weeks of August, bids fair to rival Munich's Oktoberfest. Founded in 1812, the festival draws some 400 exhibitors from the fertile Gäuboden region whose beers are sampled by around a million visitors;

as with the Oktoberfest, the festival is accompanied by a massive fun fair. The Agnes-Bernauer-Festspiel, held every four years (there is one in 1996 and then in 2000), recalls the unjust execution in 1435 of the humble peasant girl who married Duke Albrecht III (see page 107).

WÜRZBURG

Würzburg is one of the main wine-producing towns in Franconia, and it hosts several wine festivals, in particular those in the Bürgerspital, at the end of June, and the city's wine festival, at the end of September.

PILGRIMAGES

Altötting is Bavaria's major pilgrimage centre, drawing thousands of visitors each year from all parts of the world as well as Germany. They come to pray before a statue of the Virgin Mary and the Infant Jesus, carved out of limewood around 1300 and now housed in the town's Gnadenkapelle. Because smoke from innumerable candles has blackened the statue they call her the Black Madonna of Altötting.

The statue has a long history of working miracles. The first occurred in 1489 when a three-year-old child drowned in the River Inn; laid upon the altar in front of this Madonna, the toddler awoke from death. Since then the miracles have not ceased, and

candles around Altötting's massive square to pray before the Black Madonna.

there are some 2,000 *ex voto* paintings (thanking the Black Madonna for her intervention) hanging inside and outside the chapel.

Every day her chapel is crowded with pilgrims who join in worship led by

Apart from Altötting, there are hundreds of churches in Bavaria that attract pilgrims who come not only to view the statues but also to seek the relics of celebrated saints.

One of the oldest is the monastery of Benediktbeuern, founded in 789 after the Holy Roman Emperor Charlemagne had donated a relic of St Benedict.

Pilgrimages have brought prosperity to those churches fortunate enough to be endowed with a precious relic, so that sumptuous baroque buildings now shelter what were once humble and unpretentious

the Altötting clergy, but the biggest gatherings take place on Sunday evenings in summer – and, above all, on the feast of the Assumption (15 August), when crowds of pilgrims gather in the huge neo-baroque church (built in 1910 to accommodate 600 people) before processing with lighted

shrines. The greatest of these is the splendid pilgrimage church of Vierzehnheiligen (see page 122), which began as a tiny chapel and is now one of the most powerful baroque creations in Germany.

Children

*T*he pleasures offered to children in Bavaria are virtually endless. In Munich, for example, the Bavaria Filmstadt (page 32), the Deutsches Museum (page 34), the Englischer Garten (page 36), the Stadtmuseum (page 50) and the zoo in the Tierpark Hellabrun (page 61) are all likely to appeal to young visitors. For entertainment there is the Marionettentheater (Munich Marionette Theatre), based on a puppet theatre founded by 'Papa Schmid' in 1857, at Blumenstrasse 29a (performances daily, except Monday, at 3pm and 8pm; tel: 089 265712; U-Bahn 1, 2, 3 and 6 to Sendlinger Tor).

The Circus Krone, Marsstrasse 43, has been based in Munich since 1919 and performs from 25 December to 31 March on weekdays at 8pm; on Wednesday, Friday and Saturday also at 3pm; and on Sundays and holidays at 2.30pm and 6.30pm (tel: 089 558166; S-Bahn to Hackerbrücke).

Children's swings are to be found in Munich's Alte Botanischer Garten (Old Botanical Garden) and on the Theresien-wiese, and there are grassy play areas set aside in the Englischer Garten (English Garden) that testify to the Bavarians' pleasure in entertaining their youngsters.

Such treats are repeated throughout the whole of Bavaria. Augsburg, for example, has a Marionette Theatre, offering programmes for both children and adults (Spitalgasse 15; tel: 0821 434440). Young people who are hooked on motor sports should visit the

Puppets in Munich's Stadtmuseum

Watching Munich's Glockenspiel (on the Neues Rathaus tower) is a favourite pastime

Sportscar Museum Rosso Bianco at Aschaffenburg (see page 111), with its displays of classic Lancia, Porsche, Ferrari and Alfa Romeo cars.

Toys and dolls are the speciality of numerous museums throughout the region, one of the finest being the Puppenmuseum at Coburg, with its astonishing range of lifelike dolls (see page 118). Coburg also has a fairy-tale park (Märchenpark) with a children's railway, a fire-brigade museum, a beer garden (for parents and children) and bumper cars (Eisfelderstrasse 34; tel: 09568 7218; open: Easter to October daily 10am–6pm; admission charge). Equally popular is the nearby Weitramsdorf Schloss Tambach deer park (10km west of Coburg), with its 25 different wildlife species, and children's playground (tel: 09567 92290; open: 8am–6pm; admission charge). Another treat is the balloon museum at Gersthofen, which styles itself the world's ballooning centre (autobahn exit Augsburg-West; open Wednesday 2–6pm, Saturday, Sunday and holidays 10am–6pm; admission charge).

Finally, to remind youngsters of the occasional grimness of real life, take them to the school museum in Nuremberg (Panierplatz 37; tel: 0911 208387; currently closed). The school museum is moving to the Museum of Industrial Culture (tel: 2313875), which presents a history of education from the 14th century right up to the present day.

Sport

*T*he varied climate of Bavaria, its lakes, rivers and natural parks and its Alpine region have enabled the Bavarians to develop a vast range of sporting activities. All levels of skill are catered for, from the most inexperienced to Olympic-standard champions.

THE ALPINE REGIONS

Fischen and its surrounding villages, located in the southernmost part of Germany near the Hörnergruppe mountains and set beside the River Iller, are ideally placed for those who wish to swim (in its heated pool), to cycle, hike, or ride or to play mini-golf in summer, while in winter there is skiing to enjoy or curling to watch – an ancient game similar to ice hockey that is virtually one of Bavaria's national sports (information from the Verkehrsamt,

87538 Fischen in Allgäu; tel: 08326 1815).

Oberstdorf, further south, has an international figure-skating rink and 200km of summer footpaths (140km in winter), as well as tennis courts, golf courses and paragliding facilities. Here you can take climbing courses and guided mountain tours (information at the Kurverwaltung, 8980 Oberstdorf; tel: 08322 7000).

Further east, the Werdenfelser Land includes such famous Alpine resorts as Garmisch-Partenkirchen (see page 86) and Oberammergau (see page 88), as well as Mittenwald on the Upper Isar,

Golfing at Chiemsee

Hiking along the well-marked trails of the Berchtesgaden area

with its 80km of hiking paths, its swimming, tennis and squash facilities and, in season, rock climbing and skiing (information from the Kurverwaltung, Dammkarstrasse 3, 82481 Mittenwald; tel: 08823 33981). To the northeast of Mittenwald you will find the resort of Bad Tölz (see page 65), while to the southwest is the Blomberg summer toboggan run.

The Waldensee is a mecca for windsurfers, with other watersports centres on the Kochelsee, the Isar and the Loisach. Southwest of the town of Lenggries is the Brauneck hiking country. Rising from 700 to 1,700m, the Brauneck ensures snow for cross-country skiing courses and downhill ski-runs from December till Easter. The region has over 500km of signposted footpaths. Some 500 towns are encompassed within this region, offering almost every type of sporting activity including gliding at Königsdorf (information from the Kurverwaltung, 83646 Bad Tölz; tel: 08041 70071).

Further east is the Chiemsee (see page 66), with its sailing and windsurfing schools and its golf links, as well as raft trips on the River Alz. The lake and its surroundings are devoted to winter and summer sports, including winter walking tours, mountain hikes along 310km of signposted routes and covered tennis courts. The area includes the ski resort of Aschau and the Kampenwand peak, to which visitors often go after skiing to sunbathe in the snow, taking the cable railway to the summit (information from Haus des Gastes, Alte Rathausstrasse 11, Prien am Chiemsee; tel: 08051 69050).

The Berchtesgaden region (see page 66), on the border with Austria, forms the easternmost part of Bavaria's Alpine stretch. In summer you will find 240km of footpaths here, and the area is also popular for hang-gliding and kayaking; in winter, tobogganing and cross-country and Alpine skiing are the attraction. Bad Reichenhall, a little further north, has a cable car carrying climbers up to the craggy Predigstuhl, where (under one roof) there is an ice-skating rink plus tennis courts and a swimming pool.

Sporting facilities throughout Bavaria can satisfy the most energetic as well as those who like a more leisurely approach to keeping fit. At Augsburg, for example, the tourist office provides details of cycling tours in the Augsburg natural park; the city also has an 18-hole golf course, set amidst woods and lakes, to cater for this increasingly favoured sport.

The city also boasts over 200 sports clubs and gymnasiums, as well as swimming pools, ice-skating rinks and outdoor and indoor tennis courts. For the 1972 Munich Olympics, Augsburg built the first artificial canoe slalom stadium in the world.

In Franconia, Bayreuth offers a sports centre in the middle of the town, the magnificent Kreuzstein open-air swimming pool near the university, two indoor swimming pools, an airfield open to amateur pilots and gliders, tennis courts, riding schools and a mini-golf course.

Similarly Lindau, not content simply to offer visitors the sporting facilities of the Bodensee (Lake Constance), has fully automatic skittle alleys in the Gastätte Schützenhaus (Kemptener Strasse 132), a tennis club in Am Giebelbach, two international 18-hole golf courses, five lakeside swimming pools, a roller-skating rink (which also incorporates a curling centre) and a horse-riding school.

Such facilities are repeated in towns and cities throughout the free state, and what follows is merely an indication of the range on offer.

THE FICHTELGEBIRGE

The most exciting part of Franconia for sporting holidays is probably this granite mountain range, located in the northeastern part of the region between Bayreuth and the frontier with the Czech Republic. There are several delightful places here that would make an ideal base. One of them is Bischofsgrün, a glass-making town, which lies at the foot of the highest peaks of this range (the 1,053m-high Schneeberg, the 1,023m-high Ochsenkopf and the 868m-high Rudolfstein). Another is hill-sheltered Bad Berneck, at the start of the Fichtelgebirgsstrasse (the scenic B303 which runs along the valley of the Weisser Main). A third is picturesque Wunsiedel (3km north of the remarkable rock formation of Luisenburg, which was created by volcanic activity some 240 million years ago).

Virtually every kind of outdoor activity is promoted here: fishing, riding, tennis, squash, golf, swimming, windsurfing on the Weissenstädter Lake, flying, indoor ice-skating and parachuting. There are 400km of cross-country ski trails and 3,000km of marked paths (information from the tourist office, Bayreuther Strasse 4, 95686 Fichtelgebirge; tel: 09272 6255).

EASTERN BAVARIA

Regensburg is one of the main starting points for hiring boats to sail the Danube (enquire at the Regensburg Kanu-Club, 93047 Regensburg; tel: 0941 24324). The city also has an ice stadium, thermal baths and tennis and squash courts, while you can hire bicycles through the tourist office in the Rathaus (tel: 0941 507 4410).

UPPER BAVARIA

Quite apart from the Bavarian Alps, Upper Bavaria offers sports freaks impeccable facilities. The Altmühl Wildlife Park, for example, is a paradise for anglers. You can also hire a bicycle to

For the ultimate thrill, try parascending from the peaks above Schwangau

follow some of the 500km of signposted tracks. Canoes and kayaks can be used along the river and on the Rhein-Main-Donau canal, beneath the gliders that soar soundlessly over the Jura plateau (information from the Informations-zentrum, Notre Dame 1, 85072 Eichstätt; tel: 08421 6733).

Food and Drink

*B*avarians like to eat amply and well, indeed 'eating and drinking hold body and soul together' is an old saying often heard in the restaurants and pubs of Munich. This part of Germany holds pleasant surprises in store for food gourmets as well as those who enjoy the simple pleasures of 'homestyle' Bavarian cooking and a frothy brew.

Breakfast, taken between 7 and 10am, can be a complex meal, with a choice of any (or all) of boiled egg, yoghurt, fruit juice, cheeses and various slices of ham or cooked meat extensively laid out in many hotels on a groaning table and accompanied by either tea or coffee. Lunch, taken between noon and 2pm, can be an even ampler affair, with soup followed by a meatloaf or a leg of roast veal, served with potatoes or rice, usually accompanied by a salad and often followed by a rich dessert cake.

If they are going to eat out in the evening, most Bavarians do so relatively early in the evening, usually between 6pm and 9pm. Restaurants range from the characterful and inexpensive to the gourmet temples of culinary perfection with prices to match. Most restaurants display menus and prices on the wall outside or in the window. Service is included in the menu price, though a small tip is welcomed by the waiters, and the more expensive the establishment the larger the tip they expect. Many restaurants close over Christmas and New Year and for part of August.

Beer gardens serve hearty Bavarian dishes such as sausages or roast pork, and most allow you to take your own food. In unpretentious cafés all over the region you can eat similarly earthy food at keen prices – a quarter of a chicken, some *pommes frites* (chips) and a large beer will cost you less than DM12.

In most restaurants there is no minimum price charge and you can choose just one course if you prefer, rather than having to order a full meal. You will also find excellent inexpensive pizzas in Bavaria's many Italian restaurants. McDonald's, serving beer,

has also invaded this part of Germany, though not obtrusively: there are only a score of outlets in Munich.

PRICE GUIDE
The approximate cost of an à la carte meal for one person, consisting of soup and the dish of the day, excluding beer or wine, is indicated by one of the following symbols:
DM1 17–40DM
DM2 40–70DM
DM3 70DM upwards.

BAVARIAN FOOD IN MUNICH
Augustiner DM1
A huge traditional Bavarian inn, with a beer garden, at the heart of the Innenstadt, its façade dated 1897. *Neuhauser Strasse 16. Tel: 089 551 99297. Open: daily 9am–10pm.*
Bogenhauser Hof DM2
High-quality Bavarian food. *Ismaningerstrasse 85. Tel: 089 985586. Closed: Sunday.*
Halali DM2
Specialising in game and presided over by another protégé of the top Munich

Enjoying typical light refreshment in Munich's Marienplatz

chef, Eckhart Witzigmann.
Schönfeldstrasse 22. Tel: 089 285909.
Open: daily except Sunday and holidays
noon–3pm, 6pm–1am.

Hundskugel DM3
Munich's oldest restaurant, founded in
1440, offers less-fattening Bavarian food.
Hotterstrasse 18. Tel: 089 264272. Open:
daily except Sunday 11am–1am.

Königshof DM3
Noted for its rabbit dishes and wine list.
Karlspatz 25. Tel: 089 551360.

Preysing DM2
Fine hotel restaurant in the fashionable
Haidenhausen district.
Innere-Wiener-Strasse 6. Tel: 089 481015.
Open: evenings only Monday to Saturday.

Pschorr-Keller DM1
Beer garden and traditional food.
Theresienhöhe 7. Tel. 089 507004.

Ratskeller DM1
Typical town hall eatery, with a terrace.

Marienplatz 8. Tel: 089 220313.

Tantris DM3
Gourmet restaurant whose chef de
cuisine is Heinz Winkler, another former
pupil of Eckhart Witzigmann (see page
168).
Johann-Fichte-Strasse 7. Tel: 089 362061.
Open: daily except Sunday noon–3pm,
8pm–1am; evenings only on Wednesday
and Thursday.

Zum Klösterl DM2
Fashionable.
St-Anna-Strasse 2. Tel: 089 225086.
Open: daily except Sunday and holidays
5.30pm–midnight.

Zur Schwaige DM3
Typical Bavarian food served in the
superb surroundings of the south wing
of Nymphenburg Palace, or in the
restaurant's summer garden.
Schloss Nymphenburg. Tel: 089 174421.
Open: daily 10am–midnight.

NON-BAVARIAN FOOD IN MUNICH

AMERICAN
Luigi Malone's DM1
Authentic American restaurant serving T-bone steaks.
Leopoldstrasse 28a. Tel: 089 395071.

ENGLISH
Winchester Arms DM1
English pub with beer, darts, pub grub and traditional English Sunday lunch.
Maistrasse 53. Tel: 089 534530.

Choose from Austrian or Italian fare

BOHEMIAN
Goldene Stadt DM1
Traditional Bohemian food, such as sausage and dumplings.
Oberanger 44. Tel: 089 264382. Open: daily except Sunday 11.30am–3pm, 8pm–11pm.
St Wenzel DM1
Try the pancakes filled with curd cheese.
Ungererstrasse 67. Tel: 089 363666. Open: daily except Monday evening and Tuesday 11.30am–2.30pm, 6–10.30pm.

CHINESE
Tai Tung DM3
Quality restaurant in the Villa Stuck.
Prinzregentenstrasse 60. Tel: 089 47100/ 478366.

ITALIAN
Italy DM1
Lively and good value.
Leopoldstrasse 108. Tel: 089 346401. Open: daily 11.30am–midnight.

JAPANESE
Mifune DM3
Owned by the Japanese star of the TV series *Shogun*, its food is authentic.
Ismaninger Strasse 136. Tel: 089 987572. Open: daily noon–2pm, 6pm–midnight.

MEXICAN
Joe Peñas Cantina DM1
Serves excellent *fajitas* and *burritos*.
Buttermelcherstrasse 17. Tel: 089 226463. Open: daily 4pm–1am.

SOUTHEAST BAVARIA

ALTÖTTING
Zur Post DM2
An attractive and extremely comfortable hotel overlooking the central square of the town and serving excellent cuisine.
Kapellenplatz 2. Tel: 08671 5040.

BAD REICHENHALL
Hansi DM1
Serves vegetarian dishes.
Rinckstrasse 3. Tel: 08651 98310. Closed: Monday.
Steigenberger-Axelmannstein DM2
A hotel reputed for its cuisine and boasting two restaurants, one with a garden.
Salzburger Strasse 2. Tel: 08651 7770.

BAD TÖLZ
Schwaighofer DM2
A two-star restaurant with a *weinstube* (wine bar).
Markstrasse 17. Tel: 08041 2762. Closed: Wednesday.

A cool glass of beer beside the fountain in pretty Berchtesgaden

Zum alten Fährhaus DM3
In fine weather you can eat outside in the terraced garden.
An der Isarlust 1. Tel: 08041 6030. Closed: Monday and Tuesday.

BERCHTESGADEN
Hotel Geiger DM2
Set in attractive grounds and offering superb panoramas of the Alps, this hotel also offers some of the finest food in Berchtesgaden
Stanggas. Tel: 08652 9653.

CHIEMSEE
Luitpold am See DM1
Traditional family-run hotel and restaurant by the lake in Prien.
Seestrasse 110. Tel: 08051 609100.
Yachthotel Chiemsee DM2
Restaurant overlooking the lake.
Harrasserstrasse 49. Tel: 08051 6960.

LANDSHUT
Romantik-Hotel Fürstenhof DM3
Attractive hotel restaurant.
Stethaimer Strasse 3. Tel: 0871 82025.
Goldene Sonne DM1
Quaint.
Neustadt 520. Tel: 0871 23087. Closed: Friday.

PASSAU
Holiday Inn DM2
A large hotel with a good restaurant.
Bahnhofstrasse 24. Tel: 0851 59000.
Wilder Mann DM2
Claims to date back to the 12th century and offers a variety of fine food.
Rathausplatz. Tel: 0851 35071.
Schloss Ort DM1
Picturesquely situated where the rivers meet.
Ort 11. Tel: 0851 34072. Closed: Thursday.

Bavarian Food

In Bavaria the sausage is king – whether it is the little sausages of Nuremberg, the white ones of Munich or the magnificent 31cm-long Coburg sausage (its length derived from the staff carried by the statue of St Mauritius on the gable of the Rathaus).

These days, however, the king must look to his laurels. At Nuremberg the local sausages have to compete with crisply-roasted shoulders of pork (*Schäuferle*). In the lakeside restaurants fish is often a preferred delicacy. And everywhere you can find dumplings: little liver dumplings floating in meat broth, potato dumplings (*Röhe Klosse*) blended with breadcrumbs (particularly favoured in Franconia) or dumplings with wild mushrooms (*Pfferlinge mit Semmelknödel*).

In truth Bavaria boasts not one but many cuisines. In the Allgäu you can buy pastries known as *Nonnenfürzle* (literally 'nuns' farts'). Here on menus you find pasta described as *Allgäuer Knöpfle* and served with grated mountain cheese. Often Allgäu restaurants also serve pasta (*Spätzle*) with fried onions, or with pieces of bacon and sauerkraut.

Franconia's forests provide its restaurants with wild boar, while its rivers breed fresh trout and carp, not to speak of pike, barbel, eel and perch. Potatoes help to swell the stomach throughout eastern Bavaria (where they are known as *Erdäpfel* or *Erdbirn*). Pheasant and deer roam the forests until they end up cooked on eastern Bavarian tables. For pudding the locals relish a sweet dough, fried in fat and appearing on menus as *Ausgezogene*.

Munich is also becoming better known as a gastronomic centre, chiefly thanks to the influence of the Austrian master chef Eckhart Witzigmann, who brought Austrian and Hungarian traditions to Bavarian cooking and gained his restaurant three Michelin stars. He has also written influential cookbooks, and his former pupils have become chefs in several of Munich's other leading restaurants.

Seasonal as well as regional varieties add complexity to Bavarian gastronomy. *Nürnberger Hutzelbrot*, for instance, is a fruit bread originating in Nuremberg and eaten during the Christmas season. Made from pears, prunes, chopped figs, chopped dates, raisins, sultanas and chopped almonds as well as plain flour,

Sausages, the base of many Bavarian meals

Turn the other way if you're on a diet!

vanilla, sugar and a liqueur or brandy, often served buttered, it turns out to be surprisingly light.

Such a mix of ingredients in no way alarms Bavarian palates, which are used to imaginative culinary combinations. Mashed potatoes are habitually served with preserved pears, blueberries or plums. *Grüna Baggesla* means grated potatoes, mixed with eggs and finely chopped onions and then shaped into little cakes which are cooked in hot oil until they are brown and then served with apple sauce.

Equally imaginative combinations in Bavaria are onions mixed with cheese and *Gerupfter,* which is a tasty blend of camembert cheese, onions, paprika, raw egg yolks and beer!

Such dishes are rich, but there are richer ones. Perhaps to provide energy for the following day's skiing, you can dine heartily in the Alpine regions on a meal of braised veal topped with cream (*Kalbsrahmbraten*), finishing with baked apple dumplings (*Apfelknödel*) and marinated plums.

Throughout Bavaria, boiled beef served with horseradish is a common dish, or you can choose the spicy meat loaf known as *Leberkäs* (literally 'liver cheese' but in fact containing neither). And since this part of Germany abuts on to Austria, you can expect to see substantial *Wienerschnitzels* served in many restaurants.

SOUTHWEST BAVARIA

AUGSBURG
Die Ecke DM2
Game specialities deservedly top the menu at this fine restaurant.
Elias-Holl-Platz 2. Tel: 0821 510600.
Restaurant Oblinger DM2
Serves high-class food which is not too expensive.
Pfärrle 16. Tel: 0821 156051

GARMISCH-PARTENKIRCHEN
Grand-Hotel Sonnenbichl DM2
The Grand-Hotel Sonnenbichl possesses a highly regarded Blauer Salon restaurant in the popular resort of Garmisch-Partenkirchen.
Burgstrasse 97. Tel: 08821 7020.
Café Restaurant Riessersee DM1
Situated by the lake with views of Zugspitze.
Riess 6, 2km south of the town. Tel: 08221 95440. Closed: Monday.

KEMPTEN
Zum Stift DM1
Decent and cheap regional food. Zum Stift also boasts a very pleasant beer garden.
Stiftsplatz 1. Tel: 0831 22388. Closed: Monday.

LINDAU
Bayerischer Hof DM2
Quite simply the Bayerischer Hof is exquisitely situated.
Seepromenade. Tel: 08382 5055.

MEMMINGEN
Parkhotel an der Stadthalle DM2
The place to visit in Memmingen to be sure of fine food and, of course a beer garden.
Ulmerstrasse 7. Tel: 08331 87041.

CENTRAL BAVARIA

AMBERG
Casino Altdeutsche Stube DM2
Restaurant with a garden.
Schrannenplatz 8. Tel: 09621 22664. Closed: Thursday.

ANSBACH
Orangerie im Hofgarten DM2
Restaurant and garden.
Promenade 33. Tel: 0981 2170. Closed: Monday.

DINKELSBÜHL
Eisenkrug DM3
Good hotel with restaurant.
Martin-Luther-Strasse 1. Tel: 09851 57700. Closed: Monday and Tuesday.
Goldene Rose DM1
Lovely situation.
Marktplatz 4. Tel: 09851 57750.

EICHSTÄTT
Domherrenhof DM2
Rococo façade and excellent food.
Domplatz 1. Tel: 08421 6126. Closed: Monday.
Gasthof Krone DM1
Beer garden.
Domplatz 3. Tel: 08421 4406.

INGOLSTADT
Restaurant im Stadttheater DM2
Overlooks the Danube.
Schlosslände 1. Tel: 0841 35150. Closed: Monday.

NÜRNBERG
Historische Bratwurstküche von 1419 DM1
Dedicated to serving Nürnberg's spicy, finger-size pork sausages.
Zirkelschmiedgasse 26. Tel: 0911 222297. Closed: Sunday and holidays.

Bratwursthäusle bei St Sebald DM1
People come to enjoy the typical
Nuremberg architecture and cuisine,
including local sausages.
_Rathausplatz 1. Tel: 0911 227695. Closed:
Sunday and holidays._

REGENSBURG
Bishofshof am Dom DM2
Restaurant with a beer garden.
Krauterer Markt 3. Tel: 0951 59086.
Historisches Eck DM3
13th-century setting.
_Watmarkt 6. Tel: 0951 58920. Closed:
Sunday and Monday evenings._

ROTHENBURG OB DER TAUBER
Baumeisterhaus DM1
Inexpensive food served within a
Renaissance house.
Obere Schmiedgasse 3. Tel: 09861 94700.
Eisenhut DM3
Quality food in a 16th-century hotel.
Herrengasse 3. Tel: 09861 7050.
Goldener Hirsch DM2
The Goldener Hirsch has a fine panorama
from the patio.
Untere Schmiedgasse 16. Tel: 09861 7080.

WEIDEN
Europa DM2
The Europa's popularity in Weiden is due
to the superb cooking.
_Frauenrichter Strasse 17. Tel: 0961 25051.
Closed: all day Sunday, Monday lunchtime
and holidays._

NORTHERN BAVARIA

ASCHAFFENBURG
Aschaffenburger Hof DM2
The Aschaffenburger Hof can be
inexpensive providing that you choose
carefully.
Frohsinnstrasse 11. Tel: 06021 21441.

Hofgut Fasanerie DM3
Set in a park, with a beer garden.
_Bismarckallee 1. Tel: 06021 91006. Closed:
Monday and lunchtime._

BAMBERG
St Nepomuk DM2
Set in a former mill.
Obere Mühlbrücke 9. Tel: 0951 25183.
Würzburger Weinstuben DM2
Typical local food.
_Zinkenwörth 6. Tel: 0951 22667. Closed:
Tuesday evenings and all day Wednesday._

COBURG
Blankenburg DM2
Agreeable meals in the hotel's
Kräutergarten restaurant.
_Rosenauer Strasse 30. Tel: 09561 75005.
Closed: Sunday._
Coburger Tor DM3
Excellent hotel restaurant.
_Ketschendorferstrasse 22. Tel: 09561
25074. Closed: all day Friday and
Saturday lunchtime._

WÜRZBURG
Bürgerspital-Weinstuben DM1
The local wines are served with _meefischli_,
tiny fried river fish.
_Theaterstrasse 19. Tel: 0931 13861.
Closed: Tuesday._
Juliusspital DM1
This 16th-century almshouse has
atmospheric cellars where you can
sample the local wine with your food.
_Juliuspromenade 19. Tel: 0931 54080.
Closed: Wednesday._
Maritime Hotel DM3
First-class cuisine.
Pleichertorstrasse 5. Tel: 0931 30530.
Weinhaus zum Stachel DM2
Traditional fish dishes.
_Gressengasse 1. Tel: 0931 52770.
Closed: Sunday._

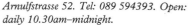
DRINK

Tradition asserts that Bavaria's first brewery was set up in 724 by the missionary St Korbinian. Certainly Bavarian monks were brewing beer in the early 14th century, and their legacy lingers on in *Starkbier* (strong beer), brewed in March and originally intended to succour the religious during the stringent days of Lent. Bavaria's brewing industry is still regulated by principles laid down by Duke Wilhelm IV in 1516, who limited the ingredients to yeast, barley, hops and water.

Munich's major beers are Hofbräu, Löwenbräu, Hackerbräu, Pschorrbräu, Spatenbräu, Paulaner-Thomasbräu and Augustinerbräu. In the city's beer cellars and gardens skilled waitresses will carry half-a-dozen or more glasses or ceramic jugs, each foaming with a litre of beer.

BEER CELLARS AND GARDENS

Among Munich's beer cellars and gardens are:

Augustinerkeller

Selling the high-quality Augustiner beer, the cellar also serves traditional Bavarian food; regulars jealously guard their own special seats, so check before you sit.

Careful balancing act

Arnulfstrasse 52. Tel: 089 594393. Open: daily 10.30am–midnight.

Biergarten am Chinesischen Turm

The popular 'Beer garden by the Chinese Pagoda' has a seating capacity of up to 7,000, making this Munich's largest beer garden.

Englischer Garten 3. Tel: 089 395028. Open: daily 10am–midnight.

Hirschau

Up to 1,000 drinkers can gather here at any one time and still there is space for those wishing to dance in the garden.

Gysslingstrasse 15. Tel: 089 369945. Open: March to November, daily except Monday 8am–1am; December to February, daily except Monday 6–11pm.

Hirschgarten

Families with children are particularly welcome.

Hirschgartenallee 1. Tel: 089 172591. Open: daily 10am–midnight.

Hofbräuhaus

The most famous beer cellar in Germany.

Am Platzl 9. Tel: 089 221676. Open: daily 8am–midnight.

Löwenbräukeller

The main outlet for one of the city's celebrated breweries.

Nymphenburgerstrasse 2. Tel: 089 526021. Open: daily 9am–11.30pm.

Salvatorkeller

Better known locally as Nockherberg, it was here that the Paulaner-Thomas brewery began the Munich tradition of brewing strong, dark beer to welcome the New Year.

Hochstrasse 7. Tel: 089 483274. Open: daily 9.30am–midnight.

Waldwirtschaft Grosshesselohe

Up to 2,000 revellers can sit down to drink here.

Georg-Kolbe-Strasse 3. Tel: 089 795088. Open: daily 11am–11pm.

Although beer is Bavaria's favourite beverage, there are some celebrated wines as well

WINE AND WINE BARS

The wines of Bavaria are cultivated in Franconia, in the easternmost vineyards of western Germany. Centring on Würzburg, grapes are grown on the slopes of the River Main and its tributaries, the main varieties being Silvaner and Müller-Thurgau. In former times these wines were all given the name *Steinwein*, named after a celebrated Würzburg vineyard. They are bottled in a green, squat flagon known as a *Bocksbeutel*.

Würzburg (see page 124) remains the major centre for sampling Franconian wines. Its most celebrated *Weinstuben* (wine bars) can be visited in the Bürgerspital (see page 129), established in the 14th century to shelter the aged and still doing so, funded by the sale of wines from its own vineyards

(Theaterstrasse 19; tel: 0931 13861).

Other good wine bars are the Hofkeller-Weinstuben (Residenzplatz 1; tel: 0931 54670, closed Sunday evening and Monday), which also boasts a beer garden, and the Juliusspital-Weinstuben (Juliuspromenade 19; tel: 0931 54080).

Naturally Munich also has its *Weinstuben*, among them the Pfälzer Weinprobierstube in the Residenz (Residenzstrasse 1; tel: 089 225628; open: daily 10am–11.30pm), the vaulted Weinstadl (Burgstrasse 5; tel: 089 221047; open: daily 10am–1am) and the Weinstube Holzbar (Frauenstrasse 10; tel: 089 224141; open: Monday to Friday 4.30pm–1am, Saturday 11am–4pm; closed on holidays), a homely, comfortable spot to taste wine and sample Swabian food.

MARKETS

Undoubtedly the most celebrated market in Bavaria is Munich's Viktualienmarkt (see page 53). With its maypole and its stalls covered with gaily coloured awnings, this has been Munich's central market since 1807. The market's three fountains are decorated with statues of Munich's best-loved humorists and singers: Karl Valentin (1882–1948), Weiss Ferdl (1882–1949) and Liesl Karlstadt (1892–1960). Its booths and shops sell local vegetables, flowers, fish, fruit, herbs, cheese and drink, as well as goods from many other countries.

Hearty, inexpensive food, washed down by beer, is sold in little taverns half-open to the elements, as well as in the Viktualienmarkt's beer garden.

The plethora of Bavaria's local markets is displayed at Regensburg, whose general market (on Kumpfmühler Strasse Wednesdays and Saturdays, closing at noon) is supplemented by a Monday and Saturday flower market on Altdorferplatz, a daily fruit and vegetable market in the Alter Kornmarkt and a potato market on weekdays in Wöhrdstrasse and Werftstrasse. Almost

Munich's central market

every city enjoys a similar number and variety of markets.

CHRISTMAS MARKETS

Every city and town worth its salt hosts a *Christkindlmarkt*, following a tradition begun in Nuremberg in the mid-16th century. From the Friday before Advent until Christmas Eve, Nuremberg's streets are festooned with garlands and lights. Children's choirs and brass bands perform beside the city's stupendous fountain. Surrounding a Christmas crib in the centre of the Hauptmarkt, fir-clad stalls sell Christmas decorations, decorated candles, local handicrafts and little figures made of dried fruit and crêpe paper called *Zwetschgenmännle* ('plum people'). Other stalls offer Nuremberg's little pork sausages and the honey and gingerbread cakes known as *Lebkuchen*, which visitors wash down with mulled red wine.

Munich's *Christkindlmarkt* lasts from the end of November to Christmas Eve and developed out of the medieval celebration of the feast of the patron saint of children, Santa Claus (St Nikolaus), which falls on 6 December. Later, the stallholders of its Viktualienmarkt cashed in on the festival and started to host a long-running Christmas fair.

Since 1972, Munich's *Christkindlmarkt* has centred on the Marienplatz and the pedestrianised zone surrounding this square. An enormous Christmas tree decked with lights dominates the square with its maze of stalls. The air is fragrant with the scent of mulled wine and burnt almonds. From late November, Advent carols are sung here, and in the week before Christmas you can enjoy Christmas carols in the monastery church of St Anna.

At Augsburg, visitors to the *Christkindlmarkt* (which starts on the Friday before Advent and ends on Christmas Eve) are likely to suffer from a surfeit of angels. In 1493 Hans Holbein the Elder painted some angel musicians for the city's cathedral high altar. Today modern *Mädchen*, winged like these angels, their long tresses curled, play lutes for the spectators at the *Christkindlmarkt*. Even Augsburg's *Lebkuchen* (Christmas cookies) are baked in the shape of angels.

Among the many other Bavarian Christmas markets, that at Rothenburg ob der Tauber is especially fine, in part simply because of the beauty of the setting. The stalls, selling candles, gingerbread cakes and every conceivable Christmas decoration, are set up in the Marktplatz, shaded by the arcaded town hall. On the Friday before Advent the Bürgermeister (Mayor) and a brass band concert inaugurate the market, after which festivities continue until 20 December. Every day either a brass band or a group of singers performs in the Marktplatz. The slender, late 14th-century basilica of St Jakob hosts concerts, as well as a special *Christkindlmarkt* service, with magnificent music, on the feast of St Nikolaus.

Every town has a market selling inexpensive and fresh local produce

Hotels and Accommodation

*B*avaria receives about one-third of all the German holidaymakers who choose to stay at home for their vacation, not to mention an equal number of travellers from abroad. As a result the total number of nights spent each year in hotels and private accommodation amounts to a staggering 94 million. To cope, the region has some 700,000 beds available in hotels and private houses. Munich alone has some 350 hotels and guest houses with over 37,000 beds. Despite this, hotels and guest houses are rarely likely to have empty rooms during the festive season or the main summer holiday period, and advance booking is necessary if you intend to visit during these periods.

The choice is wide, both in terms of price and of individual preference, beginning at the top with luxurious apartments boasting private gardens and swimming pools, and ranging down to cosy rooms with breakfast provided.

Double rooms in deluxe hotels, such as the celebrated Vier Jahreszeiten in Maximilianstrasse, Munich, start at around DM465. In a medium-price hotel double rooms start at DM200. Always enquire about special offers. Even plush hotels sometimes offer short-break packages of three nights with bed and breakfast for as little as DM219, and weekends with full board for around DM199.

Rooms are usually cheaper outside the capital (the exception being in such popular tourist spots as Oberammergau). Conveniently, you can arrange a double booking with a hotel chain, such as the luxurious Maritim (tel: 0221 924080), to spend, say, half a week in Munich and the second half in Nuremberg.

Less expensive is the Dorint chain, with its extremely well-appointed hotels in Munich-Freising, Starnberg, Würzburg, Bad Brückenau, Garmish-Partenkirchen (tel: 0800 960024). In most villiages a *Gasthof* will be surprisingly inexpensive. The sign *Zimmer frei* indicates bed and breakfast rooms.

Rural Bavaria has many a fine country inn, often with a long history of serving travellers. A bewildering series of names depicts such hostelries: *Gasthof, Gasthaus, Gaststätte, Gästehaus, Fremdenzimmer, Pension, Hotel* and *Ferien-wohnungen*. Some only serve meals and do not have rooms. The cheaper hotels generally offer hot and cold water in your room, with shared shower or bathroom facilities.

If you are exploring the country without an advance booking, make sure you start looking early enough for a bed for the night, certainly before 6pm, which is the time when inns start serving evening meals. Remember, too, that innkeepers usually take a day off during the week (the *Ruhetag*). On these rest days, you may still be able to book a room for the night, but the restaurant will be closed.

Invariably it is safer to book ahead, especially around Christmas and New Year, at Easter, during school holidays and particularly in July and August. Tourist offices all have lists of hotels. In addition, many tourist offices are happy to find and book accommodation for visitors; when you write, you should specify the price category, the kind of rooms you require and your exact vacation dates.

Ambience

Many inns, especially those in small villages, preserve such traditional features as the old and beautifully tiled stove (the *Kachelofen*), even though every room is nowadays centrally heated. If the inn is attached to a pig farm, the pork chops will be unusually succulent (look for the information *Hausschlachtung/Metzgerei*, meaning 'home butchery').

In almost every hotel and restaurant you find the traditional host's table, the *Stammtisch*. Invariably it lacks a table cloth, though the *Stammtisch* will usually be a far more elaborate and intricately carved affair than the other tables in the inn. Often a finely wrought metal ornament declares its name. Casual guests at the inn do not sit here. Instead, towards the end of an evening, the host, having checked with each guest that all is well with the meal, will sit with his friends, often playing cards.

Hotel services

Animals are welcome at hotels with the slogan *Haustiere willkommen* ('Pets welcome') and you can take them to hotels that say *Hundefreundlich*. Nearly all hotels have direct-dial telephones in their rooms. Increasingly hotels have no-smoking rooms (*Nichtraucherzimmer*). Some also offer menus to cater for special diets (*Diätkost auf Wunsch*). On a family holiday you can ask for an additional bed to be provided in your room (*Zusatzbett moglich*). An open-air swimming pool is a *Freibad* (*beheizt* if heated), an indoor swimming pool is a *Hallenbad*.

Alpine huts

Climbers and mountain hikers can double their pleasure by spending a night on the summit, watching the sun go down and waking at dawn to witness the sun rising again. The Berchtesgadener Land in particular specialises in so-called Alpine huts (which, though facilities vary, are far more comfortable than the name implies). Some offer half-board. Some simply supply beds, while others provide beds and mattresses. A few are open throughout the year, but most are open only for the three months of the summer season. Detailed information from the Berchtesgaden tourist office (83462 Berchtesgaden; tel: 08652 9670).

A traditional Bavarian *Gasthaus* (inn)

On Business

*W*ith a volume of trade worth DM183 billion and exports of over DM100 billion, Bavaria has an export economy the size of those of Switzerland and Sweden. Its principal exports are motor vehicles, followed by machinery, electrical goods and chemical products. Electrical goods, vehicles, machinery and chemical products also figure among the state's chief imports, as well as agricultural products, beer, food and clothing.

BANKING

Bavaria boasts more banks than any other German state. The largest bank, the Bayerisches Landesbank Girozentrale, is half owned by the free state itself and half by the savings banks. After Frankfurt, Munich is the largest banking centre in Germany.

BUSINESS ENTERTAINING

Most entertaining takes place in a hotel or restaurant. It is rare to be invited into someone's home for a business meal, but where this does happen (generally for an evening meal) arrive spot on time and, as an added courtesy, bring a bouquet of flowers. If there are children in the family, inexpensive presents for them are also appreciated. The meal begins with the phrase *Guten Appetit*, while 'your health' in German is either *Zum Wohl* or *Prosit*. In spite of the fact that Bavarians, like all Germans, are happy to begin work early, expect also to stay fairly late.

BUSINESS ETIQUETTE

English is a compulsory subject in German schools, with the consequence that your German business colleague will certainly speak it. Nonetheless, it is appreciated if any sales literature you may wish to hand out is in German.

Even more important is punctuality. Bavarians start work as early as 7am. There is no fixed time for lunch, which usually takes no more than half an hour. Dress, too, is important; Bavarian businessmen and women dress smartly and regard this as a sign of professionalism.

As a matter of natural courtesy you will be expected to shake hands (with all the people present) at the beginning and at the end of a business meeting, the most senior person usually offering a hand first. Equally, the custom is never to address people by their Christian name unless you are requested to. Usually you would address them formally (Frau Dr Rumpler; Herr Direktor, and so on).

CHAMBERS OF INDUSTRY AND COMMERCE

An invaluable source of information and help, the Deutsche Industrie-und-Handelskammer for Munich and Upper Bavaria is located at Max-Joseph-Strasse 2, 80535 München 34 (tel: 089 51160). Other Chambers of Industry and Commerce can be found throughout Bavaria. Among the more important are: **Altötting-Mühldorf**, Kaiser-Ludwig-Strasse 14 in Mühldorf (tel: 08638 69148); **Aschaffenburg**, Kerschensteinerstrasse 9 (tel: 06021 8186); **Augsburg**, Stettenstrasse 1 and 3 (tel: 0821 31621); **Bayreuth**, Bahnhofstrasse 25/7 (tel: 0921 8860); **Berchtesgaden region**, Münchener

Strasse 1 at Freilassing (tel: 08654 601050); **Coburg**, Schlossplatz 5 (tel: 09561 7794); **Eichstätt**, Gabrielistrasse 5 (tel: 08421 604140); **Ingolstadt**, Jesuitenstrasse 1 (tel: 0841 35091); **Lindau-Bodensee**, Maximilianstrasse 1 (tel: 08383 4094/5); **Nuremberg**, Hauptmarkt 25/7 (tel: 0911 13350); **Passau**, Nibelungstrasse 15 (tel: 0851 5071); **Regensburg**, Dr-Martin-Luther-Strasse 12 (tel: 0941 56941) and **Würzburg**, Neubaustrasse 66 (tel: 0931 3010).

CONFERENCE CENTRES
All the big hotels in Bavaria have conference centres, fully equipped with state-of-the-art technology, often also offering secretarial and translation facilities. The Hotel Stadtpark at Regensburg, for instance, has conference rooms accommodating 10 to 350 persons, and in the same city the Hotel Arcade has five such rooms and the Hotel Ibis four, in both cases accommodating 15 to 80 persons.

Augsburg has a trade-fair centre, the Schwabenhalle, which can accommodate up to 1,200 (tel: 0821 154041), as well as a congress hall in the Wittelsbacher Park, linked to Europe's highest tower hotel (tel: 0821 324 2348). The city information office (tel: 0821 502070) publishes a guide (in English and German) entirely devoted to trade fairs and congresses.

Bamberg has imaginatively transformed several historic buildings into conference centres: the Kaisersaal of the Neue Residenz (tel: 0951 56351); a former Dominican church (tel: 0951 57291, now known as the Kulturraum); and the university's Auditorium Maximum (tel: 0951 863 1210). The city's Congress Hall (tel: 0951 871199)

also hosts concerts, an additional attraction for cultured businessfolk.

Coburg's Kongresshaus Rosengarten in Berliner Platz (tel: 09561 741851) has 10 conference rooms (the largest, the Festsaal, accommodating up to 1,100), with a total of 16 variable room combinations. Conference organisers are also provided with personal offices.

Munich boasts the massive Messegelände complex, which hosts over 30 annual international exhibitions a year devoted to building, sports, electronics, tourism and so on, with a celebrated twice-yearly fashion week (for information tel: 089 51160). The city hosts some 1,000 major congresses, conventions and seminars a year.

Nuremberg actively promotes itself as a conference city, and the tourist board has a special department dealing with enquiries (tel: 0911 233620). The city's Messezentrum (tel: 0911 86060) has a main hall able to seat up to 5,000 persons. At nearby Fürth and Erlangen are equally well-equipped conference centres, respectively the Stadthalle (tel: 0911 862468) and the Heinrich-Lades-Halle (tel: 09131 862468), both seating up to 1,200 participants.

For conferences in Regensburg you can book the Dollingersaal of the Altes Rathaus (tel: 0941 507 1011) or the university's Auditorium Maximum (tel: 0941 943 2362). The city hosts a biennial trade fair in March/April specialising in consumer goods produced in eastern Bavaria.

Würzburg calls itself a 'Congress City'. The Carl-Diem Hall seats 1,750 participants (tel: 0931 37329), the Congress Centrum Würzburg can seat nearly 1,300 (tel: 0931 37372) and the Tagungszentrum Hofstuben some 400 (tel: 0931 37351).

Practical Guide

Contents

ARRIVING

Entry regulations

Visitors from European Union countries, the USA, Australia, Canada, Switzerland and New Zealand need only a valid passport to stay for up to three months. Some other nationals also need a visa – check beforehand at German embassies or consulates.

By air

Bavaria has two international airports, a small one at Nuremberg and a major one at Munich, as well as many commercial ones. International airlines operate scheduled services to Munich, while the German national airline, Lufthansa, serves both Munich and Nuremberg from major international cities.

A bus service runs the 5km route from Nuremberg airport to the city centre every 20 minutes. For flight information tel: 0911 350 6200.

Taxis to Munich's main railway station are expensive. The airport express bus (running every 20 minutes) is much cheaper, though the journey can take between 30 minutes and three hours, depending on the traffic.

The most reliable form of transport (taking around 40 minutes) is by S-Bahn 8, trains running every 20 minutes between the airport and the main railway station. For flight information tel: 089 9752 1313.

By car

Motorways run from the main ferry ports in northern France, Belgium, the Netherlands and Germany, reaching northern Bavaria via Heilbronn, central Bavaria via Augsburg and southern Bavaria via Ulm. Munich is 850km from Ostend and 995km from both Calais and Boulogne; 960km from Dunkirk, 875km from the Hook of Holland and 890km from Vlissingen.

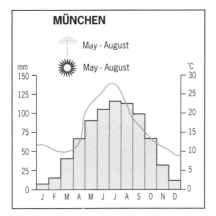

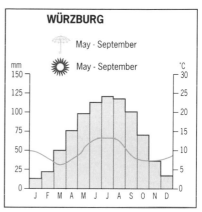

By train

Trains (with couchettes and sleepers) take 18 hours to reach Munich from Calais or Ostend. French Railways (SNCF) operate a motorail service from Paris to Munich, taking around 10 hours.

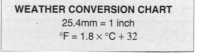

WEATHER CONVERSION CHART
25.4mm = 1 inch
$°F = 1.8 × °C + 32$

Tourist bus with route clearly displayed

CAMPING

German campsites are uniformly excellent. Apply for information to the Deutscher Camping Club, Mandlstrasse 28, Munich 80802 (tel: 089 334021). In summer many of the best sites are soon full, so book ahead, if possible. Owners of campsites are not required to insure campers for losses or theft.

CHILDREN

Children are made a great deal of in Bavaria, and you can expect to be the centre of attention if your children are well behaved.

CLIMATE

In summer visitors can expect bright skies and warm weather that is rarely so hot as to be unbearable, but be prepared for cloudy and wet days. Snow is common in winter (see also page 18).

CONVERSION TABLES
See tables opposite.

CRIME
Don't leave purses, wallets, cameras and other valuables in places where they can be stolen easily – in cars or back pockets.

CUSTOMS REGULATIONS
There is no limit to the quantity of goods that you can take in or out of Germany so long as they were purchased in another member state. There are restrictions on goods purchased free of customs duty and VAT in duty-free shops. These limits are clearly signposted. Similar limits apply to alcohol, tobacco and certain cosmetic products imported from outside the EU.

CYCLISTS
Munich's Allgemeiner Deutschen Fahrradclub (ADFC, Steingasse 17; tel: 089 480 1001) publishes maps showing cycle routes. The Munich tourist office publishes a leaflet (*Radltouren*) containing information on cycle tours of the city. Bicycles can be hired at many Bavarian railway stations. Express trains ban cycles, but they can be carried on public transport and on normal trains, so long as you buy a bicycle ticket (*Fahrradkarte*).

TRAVELLERS WITH DISABILITIES
The German National Tourist Offices (see page 189) will supply hotel lists indicating special facilities for travellers with disabilities. The central German organisation for people with disabilities is Hilfe für Behinderte, Kirchfeldstrasse 149, D-39606 Düsseldorf 1; tel: 0211 310060. For the blind, the Bayerischer Blindungsbund EV in Munich is at Arnulfstrasse 22 (near the main railway station), open Monday to Thursday 8.30am–noon and 1–3.30pm, closing on Friday at 2pm.

DRIVING
Be careful to stay in the right-hand lane except when overtaking. Outside built-up areas cars ought, by law, to travel at no more than 100kph, while in built-up areas the speed limit is 50kph. Cars with trailers are limited to 80kph on main roads and motorways. There is no speed limit on motorways (though a top speed of 130kph is recommended). Drunken drivers faces severe punishments.

At crossroads and roundabouts, unless otherwise indicated by road signs, traffic from the right has priority. Most pedestrian crossings in the cities have traffic lights which must be obeyed. Wear seatbelts in the rear and front seats. Children under 12 may not travel in the front seats of cars.

Breakdown
Germany's automobile association, the ADAC (Allgemeiner Deutscher Automobil-Club, Am Westpark 8, Munich 89373; tel: 089 767676; Nuremberg tel: 0911 551414) provides emergency assistance free of charge (you pay for any parts that need replacing). Ask for *Strassenwachthilfe* (road patrol assistance).

Documents
To drive in Bavaria you need a valid EU (pink) driving licence; you can also drive on a non-EU licence but you must carry a German translation (available at consulates and motoring organisations).

Insurance
If you hire a car, collision insurance, often called collision damage waiver or

CDW, is normally offered by the hirer, and is usually compulsory. Check with your own motor insurers before you leave, as you may be covered by your normal policy. If not, CDW is payable locally and may be as much as 50 per cent of the hiring fee. Neither CDW nor your personal travel insurance will protect you for liability arising out of an accident in a hire car, eg if you damage another vehicle or injure someone. If you are likely to hire a car, you should obtain such extra cover, preferably from your travel agent or other insurer before departure.

If you are taking your own motor vehicle on holiday, check with your motoring insurers on your cover both for damage, loss and theft of the vehicle and for liability. A Green Card is recommended. It is also possible to buy packages providing extra cover for expenses resulting from breakdowns and accidents.

ELECTRICITY
220 volts; two-pin sockets.

EMBASSIES AND CONSULATES
Canada Am Thal 29; tel: 089 222661.
Ireland Mauerkirchestrasse 1A; tel: 089 985723.
UK Bürkleinstrasse 10; tel: 089 211090.
US Königinstrasse 5; tel: 089 28880.

EMERGENCY TELEPHONE NUMBERS
Police: 110
Fire: 112
Ambulance: 19222
Medical aid: 557755
Thomas Cook travellers' cheques loss or theft: (free, 24 hours) 0130 859930.
MasterCard card loss or theft: 0130 819104.

Conversion Table

FROM	TO	MULTIPLY BY
Inches	Centimetres	2.54
Feet	Metres	0.3048
Yards	Metres	0.9144
Miles	Kilometres	1.6090
Acres	Hectares	0.4047
Gallons	Litres	4.5460
Ounces	Grams	28.35
Pounds	Grams	453.6
Pounds	Kilograms	0.4536
Tons	Tonnes	1.0160

To convert back, for example from centimetres to inches, divide by the number in the third column.

Men's Suits

UK	36	38	40	42	44	46	48
Rest of Europe	46	48	50	52	54	56	58
US	36	38	40	42	44	46	48

Dress Sizes

UK	8	10	12	14	16	18
France	36	38	40	42	44	46
Italy	38	40	42	44	46	48
Rest of Europe	34	36	38	40	42	44
US	6	8	10	12	14	16

Men's Shirts

UK	14	14.5	15	15.5	16	16.5	17
Rest of Europe	36	37	38	39/40	41	42	43
US	14	14.5	15	15.5	16	16.5	17

Men's Shoes

UK	7	7.5	8.5		9.5	10.5	11
Rest of Europe	41	42	43	44		45	46
US	8	8.5	9.5	10.5	11.5	12	

Women's Shoes

UK	4.5	5	5.5	6	6.5	7	
Rest of Europe	38	38	39	39	40	41	
US	6	6.5	7	7.5	8	8.5	

LANGUAGE

Although many Bavarians have a reasonable command of English, you will find the following words and phrases useful.

Basic words and phrases

hello	*grüss Gott*
	(far more common in Bavaria than the usual German 'guten Tag')
goodbye	*auf wiedersehen*
good morning	*guten Morgen*
good evening	*guten Abend*
please	*bitte*
many thanks	*danke schön*
yes	*ja*
no	*nein*
left	*links*
right	*rechts*
warm	*warm*
cold	*kalt*
large	*gross*
small	*klein*
cheap	*billig*
expensive	*teuer*
open	*offen*
closed	*geschlossen*
Do you speak English?	*Sprechen sie Englisch?*
I do not understand	*Ich verstehe nicht*

Numbers

1	*eins*	7	*sieben*
2	*zwei /zwo*	8	*acht*
3	*drei*	9	*neun*
4	*vier*	10	*zehn*
5	*fünf*	11	*elf*
6	*sechs*	12	*zwölf*

Days of the week

Sunday	*Sonntag*
Monday	*Montag*
Tuesday	*Dienstag*
Wednesday	*Mittwoch*
Thursday	*Donnerstag*
Friday	*Freitag*
Saturday	*Samstag (or Sonnabend)*

Months of the year

January	*Januar*
February	*Februar*
March	*März*
April	*April*
May	*Mai*
June	*Juni*
July	*Juli*
August	*August*
September	*September*
October	*Oktober*
November	*November*
December	*Dezember*

Hotels

I should like	*Ich möchte*
bathroom	*Badezimmer*
double room	*Doppelzimmer*
single room	*Einzelzimmer*
breakfast	*Frühstuck*
how much?	*Was kostet?*

HOTEL-RESERVATION

HEALTH

Visitors to forested areas should consider vaccination against tick-borne encephalitis.

EU visitors with a valid form E111 can obtain free or reduced-cost emergency medical treatment. Present the form to the local sickness insurance office to get a list of doctors and dentists in the scheme and a *Krankenschein* (sickness document) enabling you to obtain treatment. The cost of prescribed medicines obtained from a chemist is not recoverable. If you need hospital treatment the local insurance office will give you a further certificate (a *Kostenübernahmeschein*) to present to the hospital authorities. If you need urgent hospital treatment, simply show the secretariat your form E111 and the hospital will obtain the certificate on your behalf.

HITCH-HIKING

Strictly forbidden on the motorways themselves, hitch-hiking is permitted at motorway entrances (as far as the blue sign with the white motorway logo). Students can arrange a lift in advance by consulting the bulletin boards at the university *mensas* (eating places open to any student with a valid student card).

INSURANCE

You should take out personal travel insurance before leaving, from your travel agent, tour operator or insurance company. It should give adequate cover for medical expenses, loss and theft, personal liability (but liability arising from motor accidents is not usually covered – see page 183) and cancellation expenses. Always read the conditions, any exclusions and details of cover, and check that the amount of cover is adequate.

LOST PROPERTY

The lost property office in Munich is at 2 Ruppertstrasse (tel: 2331).

For property lost on railway trains or in stations contact Fundstelle der Bundesbahn, Bahnhofplatz 2 – opposite platform 26 (tel: 128 6664).

MAPS

All tourist offices provide free maps of local cities and towns, though for more detailed maps you must pay a small charge. For hiking, cycling or climbing, many bookshops offer a relatively inexpensive *Wanderkarte*, invariably with an excellent map.

MEDIA
Press

Bavaria's leading daily paper is the *Süddeutsche Zeitung*, published in Munich, which is full of useful information and which carries a listings section every day covering all the main events, with a bumper edition on Friday. *Munich Found*, Bavaria's city magazine in English, is available from most Munich newsagents.

Television

Bavaria has around 20 channels.

MONEY MATTERS

Travellers' cheques are accepted in hotels and larger restaurants but in very few shops. The same is true of credit cards; most Bavarians prefer cash. Travellers' cheques, Eurocheques and foreign currency can be changed at Thomas Cook Foreign Exchange bureaux, all post offices and at most banks. Ask whether there is a minimum charge before changing since this can be a disproportionate amount if you only want to change small sums. See also pages 188–9, for Thomas Cook services.

U-BAHN

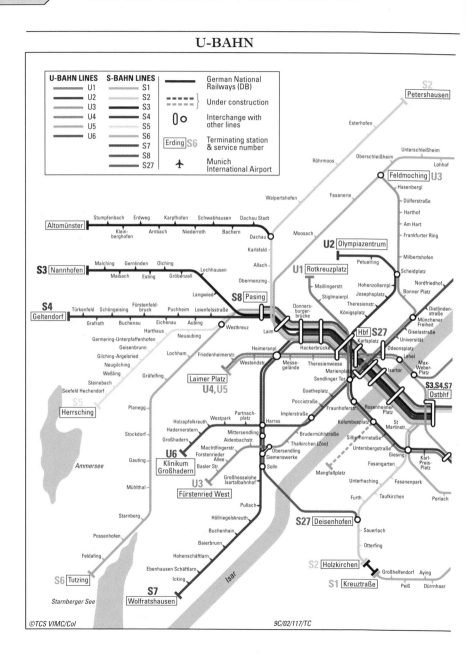

U-BAHN LINES	S-BAHN LINES		
U1	S1		German National Railways (DB)
U2	S2		
U3	S3		Under construction
U4	S4	0 o	Interchange with other lines
U5	S5		
U6	S6	Erding S6	Terminating station & service number
	S7		
	S8		Munich International Airport
	S27	✈	

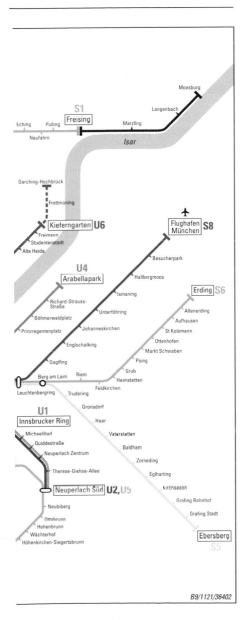

NATIONAL HOLIDAYS

1 January; 6 January (Epiphany); Shrove Tuesday; Good Friday; Easter Monday; 1 May; Ascension Day; Whit Monday; Corpus Christi; 15 August (Assumption); 3 October (Unification Day); 1 November (All Saints); National Day of Prayer (in November); 24, 25 and 26 December.

OPENING HOURS

Most shops open Monday to Friday 8.30am–5.30pm or 6pm, with late-night opening until 7.30pm on one night a week. Smaller neighbourhood stores tend to close for lunch. All shops in Bavaria close at 2pm or 2.30pm at the latest on Saturday, except for the first Saturday of the month, when city centre shops stay open till 4–6pm.

PHARMACIES

English-speaking pharmacists can be consulted at Bahnhof Apotheke, 2 Bahnhofplatz (tel: 594119) by Munich railway station.

POLICE

In an emergency telephone 110. Otherwise seek help at the nearest police station.

POST OFFICES

You will usually find the main post office – the Hauptpostamt – near to the railway station in any town. You can buy stamps in newsagents and souvenir shops.

PUBLIC TRANSPORT

In Munich, U-Bahn (underground) services are the fastest way of getting around the city centre and S-Bahn (suburban line trains) provide services to within a 40km radius of the city centre. Most other cities in Bavaria have good bus and tram networks.

B9/1121/36402

STUDENT AND YOUTH TRAVEL

Munich has a good number of young people's guest houses, such as the Haus International, 87 Elisabethstrasse (tel: 120060). The main youth hostel (Jugendherberge) is at Wendl-Dietrich-Strasse 20 (tel: 131156). Students aged 26 and under (non-students aged 22 and under), provided they are not German residents, can buy a *Tramper-Monatsticket* giving cheaper railway travel on second-class trains, or else a *DB-Junior-Tourist-Karte* (available to everyone under 26) giving nine days cheap travel.

TELEPHONES

Make international calls from boxes marked *Inland und Auslandgesprache*. The international access code is 00.

Country codes:
Australia 61; **Canada** 1; **Ireland** 353; **New Zealand** 64; **UK** 44; **US** 1.

Phone box and phonecard dispenser

THOMAS COOK

Hotel and travel services

Travellers purchasing their tickets from Thomas Cook are entitled to make hotel reservations free through any Thomas Cook travel office. All Thomas Cook travel offices offer airline tickets, re-routing and revalidation free of charge to MasterCard cardholders and to travellers who have bought their travel tickets from Thomas Cook (see page 189).

Emergencies

The Thomas Cook Worldwide Customer Promise offers free emergency assistance at any Thomas Cook office to travellers who have purchased their tickets through Thomas Cook. In addition, any MasterCard cardholder may use any Thomas Cook office to report loss or theft of their card and obtain an emergency card replacement (see page 189).

Money

To escape the hazards of carrying large amounts of cash, use Thomas Cook MasterCard travellers' cheques. For a refund of lost or stolen Thomas Cook travellers' cheques, report any loss or theft within 24 hours, dialling the free 24-hour service on: 0130 85 99 30. Emergency assistance in the case of lost or stolen Thomas Cook MasterCard travellers' cheques is also provided by Thomas Cook Reisebüro IP Reisen, Central Area Level 3, at Munich airport.

Thomas Cook in Munich

Bookings for sightseeing and excursions, foreign exchange and travellers'/Eurocheque encashment, and telephone cards, can be obtained at the Thomas Cook office in the centre of Munich at Petersplatz 10, tel: 235 0920, which is open 9.30am to 6.30pm Monday to

Friday, 10am to 2pm Saturday. Also available here is Moneygram, a quick international money transfer service.

Thomas Cook has several other offices in Munich and Bavaria, all of which provide services under the Thomas Cook Network Worldwide Customer Promise to MasterCard cardholders, Thomas Cook travellers' cheque holders and other travellers who have obtained their travel tickets from Thomas Cook; they also offer general travel services such as hotel reservations and car rental. These include branches of Thomas Cook Reisebüro at Kaiserstrasse 45, in Munich-Schwabing; Maximilianstrasse 15, Bayreuth; Kirchenstrasse 8, Tutzing. A full list can be obtained from your Thomas Cook travel consultant.

TIME
Bavaria observes Continental European Time which is one hour ahead of Greenwich Mean Time (GMT) in winter and two hours ahead in summer.

TIPPING
Though service charges are added to bills, leave the small coins in your change. A tip of 5 to 10 per cent is the norm.

TOILETS
Toiletten are marked *Damen* (women) and *Herren* (men). Often there is a small charge.

TOURIST OFFICES
Canada German National Tourist Office, 174 Bloor Street East, North Tower, Suite 604, Toronto (tel: 414/968 1510).

UK German National Tourist Office, Nightingale House, 65 Curzon Street, London W1Y 8NE (tel: 0171-493 0080).

US German National Tourist Office, 747 Third Avenue, 33rd floor, New York, NY 10017 (tel: 212/308 3300); German National Tourist Office, 444 South Flower Street, Suite 2230, Los Angeles CA 90071 (tel: 213/688 7332).

ACKNOWLEDGEMENTS
The Automobile Association wishes to thank the following organisations, libraries and photographers for their assistance in the preparation of this book.
BAVARIAN FILM SHOWS 32
MUNICH TOURIST OFFICE 149 (R Helz), 152 (C Reiter)
REX FEATURES LTD 12, 13
SPECTRUM COLOUR LIBRARY 90, 90/1, 145a
STÄDT LICHTBILDSTELLE 151
ZEFA PICTURES LTD 5, 146, 147, 153, 156b, 157a, 157c
The remaining photographs are held by the AA PHOTO LIBRARY and were taken by Antony Souter, with the exception of pages 10, 11a, 14b, 15c, 18, 68, 70, 71a, 71b, 82, 86, 87, 96, 97, 100b, 101, 102, 103, 104, 105, 106, 107, 109, 111, 114, 115, 118, 126/7, 135, 137, 139, 142, 143, 155, 167 and 175 which were taken by Adrian Baker.
The photographer would like to thank British Airways and Avis Holiday Cars for their assistance.

The author would particularly like to thank Frau Agatha Suess of the German National Tourist Office, London; Herr Markus Ruediger P R director of Lufthansa, London; Frau Brigitte Maier, PR director of the Tourist Board of Bavaria and her colleague Herr Alex Baumgartner; Frau Elke Mülhause, sales manager of Arabella Hotels; H S Bharj and A W Bentley.
The Automobile Association would also like to thank Christiane Wronski and Stewart Marshall, Thomas Cook Germany.

CONTRIBUTORS
Series adviser: Melissa Shales   Copy editor: Christopher Catling
Thanks also to James Bentley for his updating work on this revised edition.